Advanced Praise for *Conversations That Win the Complex Sale*

The Power Messaging techniques outlined in this book have been enthusiastically embraced and adopted by our sales teams, and they've elevated our game. By applying this real-world, customer-focused approach to message development and delivery, you should expect to create more deals, increase pipeline velocity, and close more business. Moreover, you will invigorate your sales force, and your salespeople will thank you. Power Messaging sticks with you, and it works.

> David Bonnette
> Group Vice President
> North America Sales
> Oracle

Power Messaging is a foundational element in our global marketing campaigns and sales training programs. We believe these concepts are at the core of engaging in customer conversations that are focused on the customers' outcomes and what they want to achieve.

> Karen Quintos
> CMO and Senior Vice President
> Dell Inc.

Power Messaging is the process my presales teams use for delivering an impactful, compelling solution message that differentiates us in the mind of the customer. The concepts outlined in this book are critical skills for building a world-class presales organization.

> Ken Hamel
> Senior Vice President
> Global Solutions and Presales
> SAP

Our new messaging, using the approaches presented in this book, is great, and it is being widely used by our sales team. We've never had a year-end sales meeting with content that was met with such widespread acceptance and enthusiasm. I admit that I entered the Power Messaging process with some skepticism, but count me as a convert!

Jerry D. Cline
Senior Vice President
Retail Sales & Marketing
AmerisourceBergen Drug Company

In a world where the status quo is not an option, the best sales professionals have become *orchestrators of change*! The best salespeople sit across the table and make change easy for their customer by creating a succinct story and vision for what to change, how to change it, and how it will affect customer results. An enterprise focus on sales messaging, using the concepts in this book, is the hidden secret to driving incremental sales productivity and overwhelming customer success!

Ken Powell
Vice President
Worldwide Sales Enablement
ADP

The Power Messaging techniques in this book are the foundation of how our marketing team creates our sales messages, as well as the process our field sales teams use for delivering that message in a unique and compelling way. Power Messaging is the foundation of success for high-performing marketing and sales organizations. At Kronos, our results are a reflection of the power of the tool.

Aron Ain
CEO
Kronos

CONVERSATIONS THAT WIN THE COMPLEX SALE

CONVERSATIONS THAT WIN THE COMPLEX SALE

Using POWER MESSAGING to
Create More Opportunities, Differentiate
Your Solutions, and Close More Deals

ERIK PETERSON
TIM RIESTERER

NEW YORK   CHICAGO   SAN FRANCISCO   LISBON   LONDON
MADRID   MEXICO CITY   MILAN   NEW DELHI   SAN JUAN
SEOUL   SINGAPORE   SYDNEY   TORONTO

The **McGraw·Hill** Companies

3 4 5 6 7 8 9   DOC/DOC   1 6 5 4 3 2

ISBN   978-0-07-175090-5 (print book)
MHID   0-07-175090-8

ISBN   978-0-07-175258-9 (e-book)
MHID   0-7-175258-7

This publication is designed to provide accurate and authoritative information in regard to the subject matter covered. It is sold with the understanding that neither the author nor the publisher is engaged in rendering legal, accounting, securities trading, or other professional services. If legal advice or other expert assistance is required, the services of a competent professional person should be sought.

   —*From a Declaration of Principles Jointly Adopted by a Committee of the American Bar Association and a Committee of Publishers and Associations*

Library of Congress Cataloging-in-Publication Data

Peterson, Erik.
   Conversations that win the complex sale : using power messaging to create more opportunities, differentiate your solutions, and close more deals / by Erik Peterson, Timothy Riesterer. — 1st ed.
      p. cm.
   ISBN 978-0-07-175090-5 (alk. paper)
   1. Sales promotion. 2. Communication in marketing. I. Riesterer, Tim. II. Title.
   HF5438.5.P484 2011
   658.8'2—dc22

                                                              2010052522

McGraw-Hill books are available at special quantity discounts to use as premiums and sales promotions or for use in corporate training programs. To contact a representative, please e-mail us at bulksales@mcgraw-hill.com.

This book is printed on acid-free paper.

CONTENTS

PART 3
YOUR POWER MESSAGE

ACKNOWLEDGMENTS

Erik Peterson

I would like to thank my wife, Christie, for making it possible for me to do a job that I love. My boys—Jeremy, Zack, and Brett—have been a constant inspiration to me. They remind me that I want this book to be something that I'll be proud to have them read someday. To my mom and dad, thank you for showing me that you don't have to accept what the world hands you. The opportunity exists for everyone to make his or her own situation, if he or she is determined enough. And to Tim, thank you for pushing (in a positive way) to finish the work. Great ideas have no impact if they aren't released to the world.

Tim Riesterer

I wish to thank the five beautiful women in my life—my wife, Laura, and my daughters, Rachel, Emily, Anna, and Hope—for their love and support and for helping me keep the "main things" . . . the main things. I thank my faith, my pastor, and my quartet singing buddies for opportunities to live a life of significance, not just success; Joe Terry for proving that one plus one does equal three; and my coauthor, Erik, for leading by example and always pushing for great.

Joint

This book has coauthors on the cover, but it really has a thousand authors. This is our best effort to bring together the collective wisdom of those who came before us. As Isaac Newton famously said, we are standing on the shoulders of giants. To CVI's founders, Chuck and Karen, thank you for creating the foundation for everything that has come since. To the other members of the CVI team, both past and present, thank you for your contribution to the content, which we've tried our best to honor here. To our thousands of customers, thank you for continuing to push us to be better.

INTRODUCTION

Messaging Fuels Methodology

It's not just about where to show up and who you
need to speak with—it's about what you say when
you get there.

n 1986, French racing driver Alain Prost tried to race the
German Grand Prix without any fuel.

Okay, that's not exactly true. Actually, Prost's car ran
out of gas on the finishing straight of the last lap. After
leading the race for most of the day, Prost wasn't going to
let this stop him. So, instead of retiring, Prost got out of his
car and tried to push it to the finish line, to great applause
from the crowd.

However, the finish line was too far, and he couldn't
reach it. He could only watch in dismay as cars that weren't
as good as his on that day passed him and beat him.

Salespeople and sales executives tell us that the same
thing is happening with their sales methodologies. They
invest in a process, but they never make it to the finish line.

One big question we always get is: "How is all this sales messaging different from a sales methodology?" This seems to be the first reaction when you start talking about changing customer conversations. Salespeople, managers, and trainers assume that they learned all that when they were trained on one of the many sales methodologies.

Our initial response is typically to ask a question: If you build the world's greatest race car, but you don't put gas in the tank, how fast will it go? Will you win any races?

It's the same with sales processes and methodologies. You can put the right structure in place for making a great sales call. But, without the right messages, tools, and coaching, process alone won't get you the victory.

You can get behind the wheel, and everything appears ready. But, you still aren't going to win unless you put fuel in the tank. Great sales messaging is the gas that makes the race car go. Messaging fuels methodology.

Put another way, sales methodology is about how to structure an opportunity or an account. It helps you create a framework for creating a deal and knowing whether you are making progress as you manage that deal through the pipeline.

But, at various points during the sales process, your lips have to move or your fingers have to hit the keyboard, and you have to execute a remarkable, memorable, and compelling customer conversation. These messaging moments of truth will mean the difference between winning and losing every time, because it's not just about knowing where to show up and whom to speak with—it's about what you say when you get there.

Dial a Methodology

When the economy is great, as it was in the late 1990s with the technology bubble, even mediocre salespeople can exceed their quota. More recently, several analyst firms have found that, on average, about 50 percent of companies' sales reps are achieving their quota. Ironically, as the economy has gotten tougher, these analysts also reported that 80 percent or more of the companies surveyed planned on raising their salespeople's quotas.

So, when Sales needs to hunker down and improve its performance, what do you typically hear from sales management? We need a better sales process. We need a better methodology.

Then, your sales management team and your sales training experts spin the dial to pick one of the many options available in the marketplace—in hopes that it will help you rise above the economic pressures and rapid commoditization of your market.

Unfortunately, many of these programs struggle to deliver the results hoped for. In fact, a few years back, McKinsey & Company documented that 75 percent of solution-selling efforts at companies were deemed to be failures within three years.

Having the right messages to fuel your methodology is more important than ever.

Four years ago, we performed a survey of marketing and sales executives for Tim's first book, *Customer Message Management: Increasing Marketing's Impact on Selling*. We found that 70 percent of the executives surveyed ranked commoditization or competitive differentiation as their number one threat to growth—outside the economy.

Why?

- There are more capable competitors than ever before.
- Customers are overwhelmed by the amount and complexity of information.

As a result, customers, in their confusion, were telling salespeople that they see all the competitors as the same. Your challenge is to avoid commoditization and set yourself apart from the competition.

Given that sales processes and methodologies have been around for 20 years, most companies have tried two or three of them, and most salespeople have been trained on at least that many, don't you think maybe something is missing?

Your sales conversations are becoming the last battleground in competitive differentiation. And, your messaging, even more than your methodology, is what matters most in this hypercompetitive environment. You could argue that your message is your most strategic competitive asset when everything else appears to be the same.

Messaging Is a Top Strategic Initiative

Recently some of the top analyst firms have done research that seems to be pointing to this same conclusion—sales messaging that fuels better customer conversations is a top strategic initiative.

In one example, Sirius Decisions, a leading marketing and sales advisory service, concluded, "The salesperson's inability to communicate value during customer interactions is perceived as the greatest inhibitor to sales success."

In a corresponding piece of research in which the firm asked executive customers about the quality of their interactions with salespeople, only 10 percent of executives rated their sales calls as providing enough value to warrant the time they spent on them.

Another major industry firm with a significant sales enablement practice, Forrester, determined that only 15 percent of sales calls add enough value, according to executives surveyed. And just 7 percent of those executives said that they would probably schedule a follow-up. Forrester added that the frustration that executives felt as a result of having their time wasted actually created a level of hostility toward the company whose salesperson made the presentation and could have a material impact on their decision.

The common theme across all of these statistics is the messaging element: what salespeople say, do, and write in order to create perceived customer value.

No Prize Money for Second Place

Unlike Alain Prost, the race car driver we mentioned at the beginning of this Introduction, who probably still finished "in the money" that day, there is no money for someone who finishes second or third in a sales cycle. So, these statistics are scary.

Thus, it would make sense that companies and salespeople have received a wake-up call and are looking at their customer conversations as a way to create a distinctive purchase experience and separate themselves from the competition.

Does your methodology improve your customer conversations? Does your sales process improve your ability to communicate value during a customer interaction?

Does your process or methodology help you to position your offerings as solutions to client problems and then differentiate them from the competition? Does it help your salespeople create a remarkable, memorable, and compelling experience when they are sending e-mails, communicating over the Web, or making an in-person presentation?

Success isn't going to be all about following the right four-, five-, or six-step process.

It's not about where you show up. It's about what you say when you get there.

A Note on the Look of the Book

All of the techniques and philosophies in this book are about conversations, not presentations. They are about being more personal than typical sterile corporate dialogues. In fact, they are often accompanied by messaging that is communicated using numbers, pictures, and charts that are drawn on notepads, flip charts, whiteboards, or even napkins. It's all part of creating an interactive consultative conversation—one in which the prospect or customer is engaged, participating, and owning the discussion, as opposed to being presented at. That's why many of the graphics in this book appear as hand-drawn, simple illustrations. Consider them a model for how you can tell your story in a way that sets you apart from everyone else with a PowerPoint.

PART 1

THE POWER OF CHANGE

CHAPTER 1

Intentions and Instincts: Why You Need This Book

B abe Ruth began his baseball career using a 54-ounce bat. That's a *big* bat. For those of you who are not familiar with what's "normal" for baseball bats, most professional baseball players today use a bat that weighs between 31 and 35 ounces.

From the beginning of his career, Ruth was a remarkable hitter. He first led the league in home runs in 1918, when he hit 11. And then he led the league in home runs in 11 of the next 13 seasons. Arguably his best hitting season was 1927, when he hit 60 home runs. He hit more home runs that season than all but two *teams*.

That year, the bat he used weighed only 40 ounces.

That's right. Even though he started his professional baseball career as a feared hitter, he didn't become the greatest hitter of his generation, and arguably the greatest hitter in history, until he dramatically changed his approach to hitting, reducing the weight of his bat by more than 25 percent.

Why did it take him so long to realize that he needed to reduce the weight of his bat?

Because it went against his instincts.

His instincts told him that to have the power he needed to hit home runs, he had to swing the heaviest bat he could carry and still make contact with a pitch.

In fact, you can understand why he would think that the heavier the bat, the better. It just makes sense, doesn't it? You must get more power from swinging a heavy bat than from swinging a light one, right? I mean, it's obvious!

It turns out that it's wrong. Most of us share that instinct, but it's wrong.

To hit for power, you also need to think about bat speed.

Now, you're not going to hit home runs with a toothpick, but most people's instincts tell them to put too much emphasis on bat weight and not enough emphasis on bat speed.

Baseball isn't the only activity where your instincts lead you down the wrong path.

There was a famous experiment in which people were assigned the task of being either a "tapper" or a "listener." The tapper's job was to tap out the tune of 1 of 25 famous songs, like "Happy Birthday." The listener's job was to guess the song that was being tapped.

Before the experiment started, the tappers were asked to predict how often the listener would guess the song correctly. The tappers predicted that the listeners would guess the song correctly about 50 percent of the time.

But when the experiment was conducted, a surprising thing happened. The listeners guessed the song correctly less than 3 percent of the time!

Why did the listeners do such a poor job? Well, it turns out that while the tappers could hear the music in their

own head, to the listeners it just sounded like a discon-
nected series of taps.

But really, this isn't about the listeners doing a poor job.
What this is really about is the bad instincts of the tappers.

It was the tappers who assumed that the listeners would
do much better. It was the tappers whose instincts were wrong.

This is a book about your sales instincts and how they
are killing you when it comes to sales. Just like Babe Ruth,
you can still be successful even though your instincts are
leading you astray. But if you want to be the best in the
world, you need to learn where your instincts are right and
where your instincts are wrong.

You see, when salespeople fail to achieve their potential,
it's almost never because they are lazy, and it's not because
they aren't doing their best.

If you're like the vast majority of the salespeople on the
planet, your intentions are great and your effort is great,
but your instincts are wrong. They are taking you down
the wrong path.

*And you are often delivering a message that your cus-
tomers just don't hear.* At least, they don't hear it the way it
sounds in your head. They don't hear the tune you're playing.

That's the core, radical idea that's at the heart of this book.

Your instincts and intentions tell you to

- Help your customers. (Good intention)
- Give your customers as much information as possible. (Bad instinct)
- Show your depth and professionalism. (Good intention)

5

- Use sophisticated language to reveal your depth. (Bad instinct)
- Build relationships with your customers. (Good intention)
- Move from agreement to agreement with your customers and never challenge their point of view. (Bad instinct)
- Deliver your message in a memorable way. (Good intention)
- Play it safe and focus on being as polished as possible. (Bad instinct)

If you can take having some of your instincts challenged...

If you can be open to hearing your message the way your customer hears it . . .

You can make a remarkable change in your sales performance.

The approach and techniques in this book have been shaped through 20 years of delivering our Power Messaging workshops. During that time, we've worked with tens of thousands of salespeople in 56 countries. The companies that use this approach range from high-tech to low-tech and have familiar names like GE, Oracle, Volvo, and Amerisource Bergen.

Here's how this book is going to help you make the changes that you will need to make if you are to succeed in today's sales world. It is divided into three sections:

What needs to change. Recognize the forces that are changing the selling environment, and learn several major new concepts for the way you approach prospects and customers. These concepts include the following:

- How to create more opportunities by bringing bad news
- Why playing 20 Questions with your prospects isn't the answer
- How to provoke your prospects to create more opportunities
- The often ignored opportunities already in your pipeline that can make all the difference
- The approach to loosening the status quo with a distinct point-of-view pitch

Finding your story. Learn why your message needs to be more than just compelling facts, and how to shape your message into a story that wins more deals. This goes beyond ordinary value propositions to give you a specific approach to finding your winning story. It includes

- How to differentiate yourself in crowded markets by finding your Value Wedge
- How to avoid parity in your value propositions by creating Power Positions
- How changing one word in your message can double the number of deals that you close
- What a great message has in common with *Star Wars* and the *Harry Potter* books

Making your story come alive. Go deeper into the science and art of customer conversations, and learn specific techniques for making yours simpler, more memorable, and compelling. Here you'll learn about

- The hammock—why your customers go there, and how it kills your conversations
- How to spike customer attention and create "wow" in your conversations
- The real decision maker in every deal and how you sell to it
- Why salespeople overuse facts and figures and how you can do better in proving your claims
- Where presentation skills training misses the point

If you're a student of these techniques, this book will give you depth that it's not always possible to get to in the two-day course, as well as a refresher on the core concepts. And we welcome you back.

If you're new to the ideas in this book, you will never look at selling the same way again.

It's time to get started.

CHAPTER 2

Overcoming the Status Quo: Your Biggest Competitor

Have you heard the ancient story of Buridan's donkey? It refers to a hypothetical situation in which a donkey is placed precisely midway between two identical piles of hay. The donkey stands there contemplating his options and is paralyzed with indecision.

Unable to make a rational decision to choose one haystack over the other, the donkey finally dies of starvation.

This, of course, is impossible to believe. A donkey that was standing between two piles of hay would not allow itself to starve to death. It would pick a pile and start eating.

The story of Buridan's donkey was used to mock a philosopher named Jean Buridan. Buridan believed that people would always choose the option that represented the greater good. If they were faced with two options that were very similar, they would wait until it was clear which one was better before picking one.

If you take this idea to its most ridiculous possible conclusion, you end up with the story of Buridan's donkey.

The problem with this is that, in general, Buridan was right. When people are faced with a choice between two things that appear very similar, they will in fact put off making a decision until it is clear to them which one is better. You've heard this referred to as "paralysis by analysis." When you're facing any kind of decision that's a bit complex, you'll put off making that decision until you're sure which choice is the best.

If you can't determine which choice is the best, and if you can put off the decision without experiencing a lot of pain (obviously dying would be so painful that you couldn't put off the decision, which is why the donkey story is ridiculous), you'll put it off every time. It's a natural human reaction—one that's backed up by good scientific research.

So in most cases, Buridan was right. And his theory illustrates what you might be doing to your prospects and customers when you speak with them. As you read in the first chapter, your intentions may be right, but your instincts concerning how to go about relating to your prospects and customers might be wrong.

Bombarding your prospects with messages on me-too products and services not only confuses them, but can leave them paralyzed with indecision.

Unsure about where they should invest their money, time, and energy, your prospects make the safest choice— no decision. Meanwhile, there is a business problem that is going unsolved.

Making No Decision Can Be Fatal for Your Pipeline and Your Revenue

When you engage a prospect in a sales process, do you see it as a linear process? At some point, it has an end. The prospect will choose either you or them (your competitor), right? Not really. The truth is that those are not the only two end points. There's another option, no decision, which is chosen all too often.

A banking technology company we worked with analyzed the number of stalled deals in its customer relationship management (CRM) system. It was able to determine that nearly 40 percent of deals were ending up with no decision. Industry average statistics placed that no decision rate at 20 to 30 percent. But, in the case of this customer, it was 40 percent. We've had other clients tell us that the number of stalled deals in their pipeline is as high as 60 percent.

The Competitive Bake-Off

The competitive bake-off can get pretty bloody. It's a pitched battle of You vs. Them. One moment you're up; the next moment you're down. Throughout the process, there's a "spec war" going on. You gain the upper hand with one feature, but the competition meets your feature and raises another.

You're trying to incrementally outmaneuver your competition. But you and your competition are often having a very similar dialogue with the prospect. It's no wonder, then, that up to 60 percent of prospects choose to stay with the status quo.

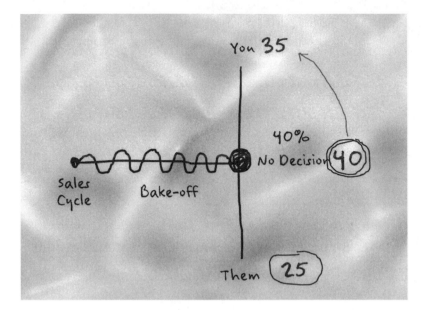

What's interesting is what happens when you put real numbers to this.

Let's go back to the banking technology company example. The company told us that out of 100 deals, it wins about 35, the competition wins about 25, and approximately 40 go to no decision. As an aside, this client also told us that this market share split has been the same for the past 10 years. The company has been battling the same competitors, trying to claw and inch its way to a higher market share, but things have more or less remained static.

So, there are two clear opportunities here. One is to take away more deals that you're losing to your competition. The other is to stay out of the dead end of no decision and win more of those prospects, as well. This book will show you how to do both.

Your battle for differentiation is often as much about changing the status quo as it is about beating your traditional rivals. [There's an exception to this rule. In a few rare instances, you might be selling a solution that virtually never ends in no decision. An example would be salespeople who sell certain types of software, such as enterprise resource planning (ERP) solutions. Once a prospect decides that he's going to buy an ERP solution, he's eventually going to pick one. However, if that's your world today, the techniques in this book will still help you.]

What do you think the odds are that you will take one of those 25 deals away from the competition? Or do you think there is a better chance that you can loosen the grip on one of the 40 that made no decision?

There's potentially more opportunity in moving prospects out of no decision than you've been able to get in the last 10 years going head to head with competitors. That's why for most salespeople, the biggest competitor is actually the status quo.

You Need a Distinct Point of View

Your first step is to realize that many of your prospects are not actually in a sales cycle, they are still determining whether they need to buy anything at all. Think of yourself as stepping back from the bloodbath that is the competitive bake-off or spec war. Instead of having a conversation that uses a competitive matrix to compare you with your competitors, you need to start having conversations that provide your prospect with a fresh insight into how she can do business better.

Senior executives tell us that the era of "playing 20 questions"—where every sales rep comes in with the usual list of assessment questions—is over. One Chief Marketing Officer (CMO) at a major technology company told us, "You'd better be able to tell me something I don't already know, about a problem I didn't even know I had, if you want to get a meeting with me."

You need to earn the right to ask questions by sharing insights. So, you'd better be prepared with insights, big ideas, or a unique perspective—whatever you call it, you'd better get some.

This book will go into specific detail on how your conversations need to change. And it will provide numerous techniques, examples, and exercises to help you make that change. One of the first concepts you will learn is how to find your distinct point of view. This will help you beat your competition and stay out of the no-man's-land that is no decision.

A *distinct point of view* is a well-choreographed prospect conversation that is designed to grab the prospect's attention, challenge his current assumptions, and convince him to consider making a change.

It's a deliberate approach to changing your customer conversations in a way that puts you in the position of sharing useful insights. It helps your customer see around the corner at what challenges are headed his way and provides him with a way out. Consider this your "distinct-point-of-view" pitch.

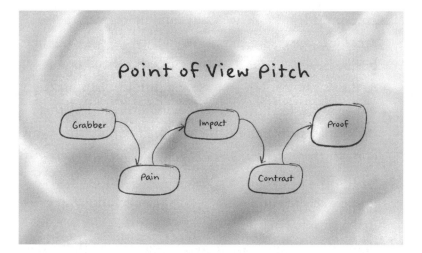

Here's a quick overview of the distinct-point-of-view concept. It contains five important components:

1. **Grabber.** Share a key industry fact or finding that is relevant to a core business objective, but that is new and fresh to the prospect. Use it to create engagement and dialogue about what the prospect is seeing in her business. It will also become a third-party validation point for the rest of your point of view.
2. **Pain.** Shock your prospect by telling her of an unknown or underappreciated problem that is threatening her core business objective. Show her how this problem may be putting her strategic objectives at risk, or how her company might be missing out on a bigger opportunity. The key is linking this to something that will get you a seat at the executive decision-making table.

3. **Impact.** Identify the closeness and urgency of the problem. Make sure that you quantify the personal, business, and financial impact of ignoring the problem or the upside of doing something differently. Your customer needs to know that the world is changing, that the changes are coming fast, and that neither the status quo nor the current vendor is going to get her there.

4. **Contrast.** Present a new way to look at or address the problem that is implicitly tied to your solution, and make sure to contrast it with the way your prospect is doing things today. Align your unique strengths as the best way to solve the problem and eliminate the pain. But, be clear about how this is different enough from the way the prospect is doing things today that it is necessary to consider making a change.

5. **Proof.** Rebuild the prospect's confidence by sharing a quick story that shows a before-and-after situation in which you helped a similar company by implementing your new way of solving the problem.

This approach moves you out and to the left of the bake-off and puts you in a position of guiding the customer buying cycle. It enables you to change the entire trajectory of the customer conversation, the opportunity, and the deal (see image). You are now advancing up and to the right rather than wading directly into the bake-off battle. In doing so, you are changing the status quo to favor you and your point of view. And you are separating yourself significantly from your traditional competitors because you've taken the prospect conversation to an entirely different level.

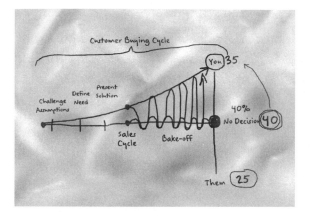

If you want a real-life example that's close to you, reread the start of this book. We've applied all of these techniques to challenge your assumptions about your selling conversations. We showed you that the way you are doing things today is putting you *at parity* with your competition and threatening your ability to win more business.

And now we've begun to map out a new way for you to approach your conversations. Our promise is that the rest of this book will be a powerful "how-to" that will change everything about the way you sell today. To give you a sense of the impact of these techniques consider what happened at ADP.

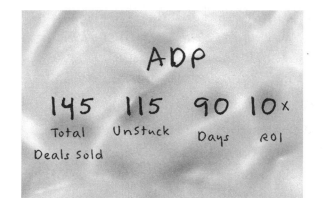

After going through our process for changing customer conversations, ADP decided to test its new point of view and conversation skills in one of the toughest possible environments—*stalled deals*. You know, the ones where a lot of energy has been expended, but the customer isn't buying and the opportunity looks doomed to die.

ADP had a significant amount of stalled deals identified inside its CRM system. These were deals in which a sales rep had already met with the prospect and pitched his solution, and had seen enough interest to lead him to put the opportunity into his sales pipeline. And then nothing happened.

It wasn't that no one was taking action. The sales reps were following up with the prospects, but the *prospects* weren't taking action. The deals were stalled. So ADP decided to target these deals using the new customer conversation approach. Using the new approach (both a new message and new messaging techniques), the sales reps were able to close 145 new customers, of these 115 were previously stalled deals, in just 90 days. This generated a return of up to 10 times the project investment and resulted in millions of dollars in revenue that had pretty much been considered lost. Let's walk through the approach together.

ADP was making a transition from providing point services for payroll, benefits, and other back-office support to becoming more of a business process outsourcing company. However, its message and its presentations were still focused on its products and services.

What the company needed was the ability to paint an executive-level picture about the value of outsourcing noncore activities. Instead of promoting the features of the services that ADP provides, we worked with the company to create and deliver messages that spoke about the pains associated with companies trying to do this for themselves, and the risks involved with doing it on their own.

Amplify Pains That Challenge the Status Quo

Here's a quick, high-level overview of how the conversation changed:

1. *Regulatory compliance.* How can individual companies keep up with the pace of changes in government rules and policies and ensure that their staff members have the knowledge and expertise to implement these changes and enforce the rules and policies according to the law?

   Solution: ADP was able to position itself as an expert that can eliminate the risk of noncompliance, which convinced companies that they couldn't maintain the in-house resources to provide the same level of assurance.

2. *Technology obsolescence and operating costs.* The tools and systems used to manage these critical back-office applications are changing rapidly, leaving many companies in a position where they can't keep up.

   Solution: ADP positioned itself as taking both the responsibility and the cost burden off its customers' hands, freeing them to invest resources in the

19

personnel and programs needed for their core business.

ADP didn't introduce new products or services; it simply changed the conversation away from itself and its offerings to one that focused on the customers and their critical business needs.

If changing your conversations can have this much impact on the status quo or no decision deals, imagine how much impact it could have on an active customer buying cycle.

You've seen the impact of no decision on your selling efforts. You need to offer a distinct point of view to get customers to care enough to do something different, and start leading them on a path to choosing you.

This will help you rise above the competitive bake-off and change the game on your competitors who are still fighting the bloody features and functions war.

The next chapter will take you even deeper by providing you with a specific approach and examples for changing the status quo.

CHAPTER 3

Bring a Little Bad News: If You Want Them to Care

If you're like most sales professionals, your intuition tells you that your job is to always keep the client happy. You think a successful client relationship is one in which everyone is always smiling.

You spend a lot of energy trying to maintain a happy equilibrium, as if the client relationship, and whether you are well liked, is the endgame. Maybe you are subconsciously thinking that if the client really likes you—you remember his birthday, you ask about his kids, and he sees you busting your hump to resolve any issues quickly—he'll throw you the next piece of business. Certainly, that can happen sometimes.

One thing is for sure: your client will typically milk this relationship for all he can get. He'll take everything you can give, for free. And, in turn, he will be very friendly. Your client reviews will come back glowing in terms of the great service you provide.

Then, one day you are caught completely off guard when you hear that your great client is piloting a concept with one of your competitors. "Don't worry," you're told.

"It's just a small side project that the senior executives asked for because they were at some conference and heard about a new approach that supposedly addresses some problems that we didn't even know needed fixing."

What just happened?

Deliberately Provoking the Client

Someone else was willing to challenge your customer's status quo.

If you learned anything from the last chapter, you know that you must be willing to challenge your customers' current situation if you are going to get them to do something different. The point here is: if you don't do it, someone else will.

Someone other than you will get the senior executives' attention by telling them something that they didn't know, about a problem they didn't know they had.

In other words, someone else will be able to gain strategic executive altitude and wrest your client's attention away from you by *bringing your client some bad news.*

In this chapter, you're going to learn how to take the next step in challenging the status quo. You'll see specific examples of how your conversations need to change in order to get your prospects to do something different.

These characteristics need to form the foundation of your customer conversations moving forward:

- You must be willing to push your prospect out of her comfort zone.

- You need to help your prospect see her competitive challenges in a new light.
- You have to highlight specific painful situations and make them unmistakably urgent.
- You need the guts to create constructive tension and use it to your advantage.

This is counterintuitive to many companies and salespeople, who are afraid that the customer will shoot the messenger and put all of your current business at risk.

It's true that throughout history, messengers have been vulnerable to attack. In ancient times, when a war was going on, news of that war would be carried by fast runners who were sent to battle fronts to report on victory or defeat, or to request reinforcements. If the news was not good, and the receiver chose to vent his anger, these messengers could meet an untimely and violent death.

But, in today's hypercompetitive, increasingly complex selling environment, you need to cut through the clutter of sameness and overcome rising risk aversion to get your customer to care about your message. To do that, you might have to be the bearer of a little bad news. What's going to make your outcome different from that of the messengers of old is that you'll also provide the fix.

A March 2009 *Harvard Business Review* article entitled, "In a Downturn, Provoke Your Customers," captured the essence of this concept and coined the phrase "provocation-based selling."

Briefly stated, the provocation concept contained three components:

- *Identify a critical problem facing your customer.*
  It should be a problem that is so ominous that, even
  in a downturn, the customer will find the money to
  address it. (You might think you'll never find something like this. But you can. We've worked with hundreds of companies, and you can always find it. You'll
  see how.) Critical problems meet the following criteria:
  they seriously jeopardize your customers' ability to
  compete, they've proved stubborn to solve, and you are
  a credible source of advice on them.
- *Formulate a provocative view of the problem.* You
  need a fresh perspective that frames the problem in a
  jarring new light. Rather than finding out how your
  client's executives currently view the problem that
  you've identified, you determine how they *should*
  view it and deliver insight on that.
- *Lodge your provocation.* To win support, convey
  the magnitude, difficulty, and urgency of the problem
  to an executive who has the power to approve the solution that you're proposing—without putting him on the
  defensive. First, you may have to convince a sponsor/
  referrer of the idea and get her to make an introduction.

Your instant reaction to the idea of provoking your
customers might be that they will view this behavior as a
negative. However, provoking or challenging your customers and prospects is not the same as being a jerk. When
this is done right, the value and insight that your customer
gets from being challenged will raise her opinion of you. It's
what the most successful salespeople are doing today.

In fact, the risks of *not* provoking your prospect are much greater than the risks of provoking him. A safe, familiar message is a forgotten message.

Hundred-Year-Old X-ray Technology

Here's an example of how this approach worked for a product that was viewed as a commodity.

We work with a client that manufactures medical X-ray equipment. It has been well over 100 years since X-rays were first used to diagnose diseases in patients. Since then, many sexier medical imaging technologies have been invented, such as CT (computed tomography) and MRI (magnetic resonance imaging), which provide impressive 3D views of the inside of your body, including soft tissue.

Meanwhile, X-rays, because of their relatively low cost and lower radiation, have retained their role as a workhorse screening tool, but patients are often referred for additional CT or MRI studies to confirm a potential diagnosis.

Imagine that you make X-ray equipment, and you have developed breakthrough advances that enable this equipment to perform procedures similar to those performed by CT. However, your hospital customers have a lot of money tied up in their CT systems. CT has become a cash cow, and it is perceived by doctors and patients alike to be the more sophisticated procedure.

How do you get the market to reconsider X-rays as an alternative to sending patients to CT in this environment? You launch a provocation:

1. *Question the status quo.* Share industry facts that get the customer to rethink the idea that CT is the only way to perform certain procedures.

   In this case, you need to point out that concerns about health-care costs make it harder to do more expensive exams, and declining reimbursements require the prospect to look for lower-cost alternatives. In addition, there are increasing government regulatory issues and concerns over the amount of radiation delivered by CT exams. The result has been a steady decline in CT procedures in the last couple of years.

   Without telling your customers that they are stupid or wrong, you need to carefully state a challenge to the current status quo. Using third-party data or information is helpful here, because it forces customers to see the challenge to the status quo coming from outside forces that they must reckon with, instead of seeing you as simply trying to force a change because you have a new widget to sell.

2. *Redefine the situation.* Next, get your customers to imagine an alternative that they may not have considered. One way to do that is to ask a provocative question that gets them to imagine themselves doing something different. In this case, you might ask

   > What if you could get the same exam done, with similar effectiveness, for 90-percent lower cost, with a 95-percent lower dose, and in one-third the time it takes to make a diagnosis?

   The key is redefining the situation in a way that offers a clear contrast to the current approach. You'll learn more about the use of contrast in later chapters in this book. But in this case, you need to quickly establish contrast between the way your customers are doing something today and the way that you propose they do it. Your customers need to see enough reason to even consider doing something different.

3. *Present an alternative.* The next step is to show your customers that there is a viable alternative that can help them respond to the changing status quo and meet the new needs that you have just established. It could sound something like this. (Excuse the jargon here. If you were the target customer, you'd understand some of the more technical terms.)

> Recent clinical trials have demonstrated that advanced X-ray capabilities can produce images as diagnostically useful as CT. And this can be done in a variety of applications, including 3D tomography and soft tissue exams. These X-ray exams can be performed for 90-percent lower cost and with a 95-percent lower dose than the CT equivalent, and doctors can read the exams in one-third the time.
>
> When you buy a new piece of X-ray equipment, it is a fifteen-year investment. Over the next five to seven years, the number of advanced X-ray applications and hospitals performing them are projected to increase tenfold. In fact, more than 75 clinical papers on advanced X-ray applications are being presented at the upcoming conference.

4. *Align your solution.* Now customers are finally in a position to care about the subtle technology advantage that separates your solution from your competitors'. Too

many times you want to blurt out the feature, but you must be patient to make sure that the customers have been sufficiently provoked to want to hear about it, and that you have led them directly to your strength:

> Only our company has developed an X-ray detector that can acquire digital X-ray images in *microseconds*—the speed needed to perform these advanced applications. All other X-ray detectors take images in *multi*seconds, which isn't fast enough.
>
> So, as you consider replacing your existing X-ray equipment, you will need a system that has the capacity to grow to meet the changing market demands. In fact, more than 40 percent of the systems that we are shipping today are going out with these advanced applications included.

Context Makes Your Customer Care

What really makes the type of provocative selling approach used in this example work is the context. Too many salespeople want to lead with the strengths of their product or service. The problem is that the customer isn't ready to hear about them. He has no frame of reference to put those strengths of yours into a situation that he feels is uniquely his.

Your customers' predisposition is to assume that all competitors are the same, and they do not want to have to change what they are doing. So, you need to create a sense of urgency around your solution, and this is accomplished by establishing a context that turns a seemingly innocuous capability into something that they can't live without.

It's just like what happens in Tim's neighborhood.

Every Saturday, a siren goes off in Tim's quiet suburban community, signaling that it is noontime. No one gives it much attention around town. It's just the "noon whistle," they often say.

But the same siren that signals that it is noon on a Saturday is also used to signal a severe weather emergency. As a result, the same siren that is ignored on Saturdays at noon, when the weather is nice, can clear an entire park within minutes on a threatening summer Saturday with dark clouds approaching.

In other words, the exact same siren, using the exact same sound, leads to a completely different reaction depending on the context. On a sunny Saturday at noon, the siren means nothing to Tim and his neighbors. It's unnecessary and unheeded. However, when there is a stormy sky or high wind, the same siren means, "Take shelter now!" Context gives the siren meaning and urgency.

It's the same with your sales message. You need to establish the right context to create urgency. It's not your product that makes the customer care. It's the changing context that makes it meaningful and gets the customer to consider doing something different.

Without the threat of unidentified problems and under-appreciated challenges, your products and services, and your features and benefits statements, sound like the same old generic gobbledygook.

If you can put your solutions in a provocative context that threatens your customer's status quo and puts her at a potential competitive disadvantage, you'll see a completely different reaction. You need to bring a little bad weather or bad news to get her to care.

Too many salespeople tell their story in a generic way, often comparing their products or services to those of their competitors and hoping that the prospect will care. But, there's no reason for a prospect to do anything different if he doesn't understand the potential impact on him.

It's just like the siren on a sunny day or a cloudy day. Instead of trying to force your prospects to understand and care about the details of your offer, you need to clearly show them the potential upside or downside of responding to or ignoring the challenges that they face.

This has never been more important for a salesperson. The Great Recession has left its mark on buyers. Just as the sting of the Great Depression haunted our grandparents and great-grandparents for the rest of their lives, the Great Recession is creating a fundamental shift in how buyers view change. It's become harder than ever to create demand and create urgency just to build a respectable pipeline.

We recently spoke with a vice president of sales at one of the biggest software companies. He said that his salespeople are spending significantly more time on "deal creation" than running traditional competitive sales cycles. "Otherwise, they'd have nothing to do," he said.

"Unfortunately, it's the part of the job they like the least, where they have the least messaging and least training," he added. "But they know they have to do it if they are to have any chance of succeeding."

If you wait for Marketing to create awareness and then demand, and focus your selling efforts exclusively on managing BANT (budget, authority, need, timing)-qualified leads, you are going to hear a lot of crickets chirping on your pipeline calls.

One superstar salesperson recently told us, "If I had to feed my children based on waiting for Marketing leads, they'd starve." That's why he approaches demand generation as a significant part of the job. This requires being provocative—bringing a little bad news to get customers to see that change is coming, and it's coming fast.

And, you're the messenger.

Your customers are looking for you to tell them something that they don't already know, about a problem that they didn't know they had. Trust us, they won't shoot the messenger. Take your messenger role seriously. Provoking and challenging your customers will be rewarded.

Example: Volvo Trucks

Here's another example to help you see the impact of learning a new approach to your messages to your prospects.

Volvo Trucks redesigned its messages and the way it delivers its selling conversations using the approaches you will read about in this book. The result was a breakthrough that moved its prospects away from the view that all truck manufacturers are the same. Of course, if your prospects see you and your competition as the same, you end up having to compete on the only thing that's left to differentiate you—price.

The new messages shifted Volvo's sales pitch from selling on the value of the trucks' features to teaching customers the value of relieving previously unrecognized needs and problems. By telling customers something about themselves that they didn't know and unveiling a series of issues that were costing customers money, Volvo was able to align its unique strengths as the best solution.

Here's how it worked. Volvo had previously emphasized the features of its tractor cabs, including the windshield size, the engine block placement, and a list of other creature comforts. It led with these strengths. What the company discovered was that this usually translated into a "spec war" with its competitors.

So, we got both Sales and Marketing into a room to create a more urgent business context for customers that would lead to Volvo's strengths and get the customers to care about the differences.

This resulted in a whole new conversation about fleet productivity. The decision makers who buy fleets of trucks needed a reason to care about cab features. The first step was discovering a link between fleet productivity and driver turnover. It turns out that the average driver turnover is really high, and it is very costly to fleet managers.

Then, Volvo connected the dots between driver turnover and the drivers' satisfaction with their work environment.

You can probably see where this is going. The number one work environment issue was the drivers' satisfaction with their trucks.

Volvo was able to show how the specific advantages they built into their trucks eliminated the top causes of dissatisfaction among drivers, and they introduced some new things that drivers really liked compared to other trucks that were on the market.

Armed with a new story about fleet productivity, driver turnover, and how Volvo was the number one truck for driver satisfaction, the company's salespeople completely changed the context of the conversation and created a differentiated dialogue where there had been perceived parity.

They turned the conversation into a business discussion about how driver satisfaction affects turnover, and how turnover affects productivity and profitability. When the conversation was refocused on key customer objectives such as productivity and profitability, and highlighted a major pain point that was threatening customers' success, such as driver turnover, Volvo was able to elevate its driver satisfaction features and rankings to a strategic necessity, instead of a traditional feature list and competitive matrix comparison.

The result was that the sales reps' confidence shot up significantly, because they now had compelling narratives for their sales interactions, which they used to create and capture more and better business despite industry pressures.

Volvo also was able to measure improvement in terms of performance. *Sales rep cycle time* (the length of time required for a deal) went down by 25 to 30 percent, and pricing premiums went up by 3 percent. This was a significant improvement in margin for this industry. When you have a message that drives more deals, increases the velocity of deals through your pipeline, and increases your margins, you know you've got a great message.

In this chapter, you've learned that just being someone who keeps her customers happy all the time is not enough. You need to be provocative, challenging your customers to rethink their status quo. And this means being willing to bring some bad news to your customers about their current situation.

This concludes the first part of the book. Now, you know why you need to change your own status quo regarding your customer conversations. In the rest of the book, you will learn a series of specific techniques to transform your customer conversations from commoditized and forgettable to remarkable, memorable, and compelling.

PART 2

THE POWER OF STORY

CHAPTER 4

Everyone Lives in Stories: Even Your Buyers

The first part of this book set the stage for how you need to change your customer conversations in order to win more sales. Since your prospects assume that you are the same as your competitors until you prove otherwise, it is up to you to make that distinction.

Here's where you get into more of the "how to" of the book. How can you deliver a distinct point of view that your prospects and customers find compelling, giving you a competitive edge?

First, your message shouldn't just be a set of facts and figures. It needs to be a story. You probably have a company story that you tell today. What's in your story?

When the typical sales professional answers that question, he uses words like *heritage, mission, vision, commitment, brand, value,* and *customer successes*. These are all part of your story.

Your story is largely responsible for attracting talent to your company and turning that talent into loyal employees.

It is also how you attract prospects to your doors and turn them into customers.

And that's good.

The challenge is that, if you're like most companies in the world today, you tell your story in a way that doesn't differentiate you much, if it does so at all.

We have a running bet that we can guess what are the first five slides in every corporate slide deck in the world. (Yours may be the exception. If so, well done!)

First, you have your Welcome slide. Then, you have your Agenda slide, where it says that you're going to give a Corporate Overview. Then, you have your Company slide, which shows how many employees you have, how long you've been in business, the size of your company, and other such information. Then, you have your Map slide, which shows a picture of all the places around the world that you support, and maybe even a picture of your corporate headquarters.

And then, look out! Here it comes! The big one! It's used so often by so many business-to-business (B2B) salespeople that a customer can feel it coming, just like you can feel the rumble of a freight train pulling up the back of a deep hill before you ever see it. Boom! The Logo slide—showing every customer you ever did business with.

Are we close? Have you ever seen a sales deck that started like that?

There are two problems with taking that approach to telling your story. The first problem is that you sound just like every other vendor your prospect has ever seen.

The second problem is, *who* is the central character in that story?

The central character in that story is your company.

But who *should* be the central character in the story you tell to prospects?

It should be your prospect, obviously.

The story your company is probably telling today is the story of who it is, what it does, who it has helped, and how it has helped them. As a sales professional, you learn your company's story and then go tell it to prospective customers. You start to imagine that if your prospects knew as much about your company and its solutions as you do, they would buy from you, right?

Is there anything wrong with that? All sales professionals sell that way, don't they?

Actually, there is something wrong with that, and it has to do with the difference between your brand message and your field message.

Your brand message tends to be a story about you. However, your field message should be a story about your prospect.

Dating provides a good analogy for the difference between brand messaging and field messaging.

Go back to the time in your life when you were dating. Think of your brand as the clothes you wore, your hairstyle, the perfume or cologne you put on, or perhaps the car you drove. (Once, when Erik was talking about this to an international group, a woman shouted out, "Don't forget the shoes!" OK—so don't forget the shoes.)

Collectively, these things represent your brand and are designed to attract another person into a relationship with you. Your corporate brand has the same purpose.

Now, what happens to you when you go out on your first date and your brand message does not turn into a field message? You keep talking about yourself and talking about yourself and talking about yourself. Your date will later tell his friends, "What a conceited, self-centered, egotistical person. All she talked about was herself." There won't be a second date.

Yet, if you really listen to most salespeople's messages, you'd hear them making the same mistake.

You don't want to do that. You want to find a way to make the story be about the prospect.

Why is it important for you to translate this story about you into a story about your prospect?

The answer lies in how the human brain works.

Humans live in story. Your story is the window through which you look at the world. It affects how you make decisions and the decisions you make. Your story is your worldview. It's the filter you use to interpret information.

You can easily think of cases in which you and a friend have looked at the same set of facts and interpreted those facts very differently.

Story is so powerful that you'll warp facts to fit your worldview.

In 2004, Emory University did a study with staunch Democrats and Republicans. These folks live in a story that says that their party is right, good, and true. They also believe that the other party is wrong and dishonest.

The researchers asked these two groups of people to evaluate information that "threatened their preferred candidate prior to the 2004 presidential election." They were in machines called *fMRIs* (*functional magnetic resonance imaging*) that can scan your brain as you make decisions. The images produced by these machines can literally show researchers where the brain is processing information and how it reacts to the inputs.

The groups were given pairs of statements from both President George W. Bush and Senator John Kerry that clearly contradicted each other. Then, they were given statements that might explain away the contradiction.

The brain scans showed that each group "consistently denied obvious contradictions for their own candidate, but detected contradictions in the opposing candidate."

Why did this happen?

It happened because the story that you live in is powerful. When you have a deeply held worldview, facts won't sway your viewpoint.

How Story Works in Selling

Imagine that you are a sea captain living in Western Europe in the early fourteenth century, before the Age of Discovery, before Columbus discovered the New World.

Today, your long-range planning tool is a spyglass— a little telescope that you can pull out of your pocket and extend so that you can see far distances. It helps you determine what obstacles there are on the horizon, and it gives you enough time to avoid them. You're happy with it. It has worked for you for many years.

Now, imagine that there's an inventor who happens to be living during the same period. He has discovered a great new navigational technology—the compass. As the inventor thinks about all the things a sea captain could do with this new compass, he gets excited about the idea that with this new technology, a sea captain could choose to sail due west and maybe discover a new world.

So he brings the compass to you and other prospects and says, "With this new invention, you can sail your ship due west and maybe discover a new world." Would you be sold? Probably not.

Why? What did most sea captains believe before the Age of Discovery, before Columbus discovered the New World?

They believed that the world was flat. And if you believe in a flat-world story, then this inventor is saying that if you buy his technology, he's going to get you killed!

Now, here's an important thing to understand. The sea captain is wrong. The world isn't flat.

But it doesn't matter.

You could try to convince him that he's wrong—that the world is round, not flat. You could tell him how you've taken measurements of the angle of sunlight at different latitudes and longitudes to prove that the world is round. You could give him the whole rational, logical, evidence-based reasons why the earth is round. But you still wouldn't sell him a compass.

As you go through this book, you're going to be consistently told that you need to challenge your customers. And you do.

You also need to know precisely how to position yourself and how far you can take that challenge. You have to challenge them as far as you can without getting outside of their worldview, whether their worldview is that the world is flat or that their political party is always right. When you find that balance, you will give yourself an unfair competitive advantage over your competition.

So, how could this inventor sell his compasses to the sea captains?

What if the inventor came to you and said, "Today, you make your money by sailing your ship from Western Europe down the coast of Africa, picking up goods, and bringing them back to Europe to sell.

"You do everything you can to make that trip as fast as possible. You keep your ship in good working condition. You hire the best crew. You constantly apply new knowledge to make the trip faster, because the more trips you can make in a year, the more money you can make.

"And, your competition does the same.

"But there's one big limiting factor on how fast you can sail down the coast. Today, during the day, you need to keep your ship within sight of the coastline, so that you always know where you are on the ocean. And because the coastline is jagged, that means that you aren't sailing in a straight line. And at night, if the sky is overcast, you have to drop anchor, because you can't see the stars to navigate by. All of this adds time to your trip.

"Now, what if you could sail in a much straighter line from Europe to Africa and back? And what if you could do it at daytime or at night and, regardless of the weather, always know exactly where you were on the ocean? And what if, by doing that, you could shave days, weeks, maybe even a month off your trip compared to your competition?"

Would the inventor sell more compasses if he took that approach? Obviously he would.

Your job is to take the story that you tell and make it a story about your prospect that provokes him to see the world differently, while also being a story that makes him feel that moving forward with your solution is the surest and safest thing that he could do.

And there's a proven process for finding that story. In the next chapter, you'll learn how to find your story by viewing it through three distinct filters.

CHAPTER 5

Finding Your Story:
The Value Wedge

S o, where do you find your story—your distinct point of view?

The best way is to do this.

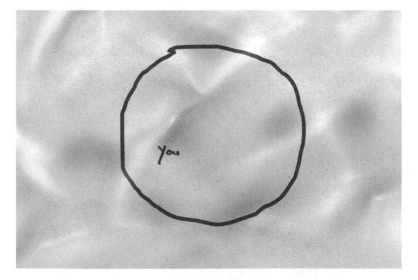

Imagine that this you circle represents your world and everything that you could possibly sell to a customer as a sales rep for your company.

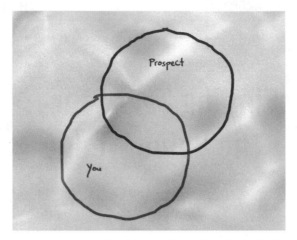

Imagine that the prospect circle represents your prospect's world—everything related to business that your prospect wants, needs, and desires. Now, when you're looking at the situation this way, where should you focus your messaging efforts? In the overlap, obviously.

And if this were your selling situation, it would be a pretty good one. But it isn't. Why? Because you have competition, and your competition has its own circle.

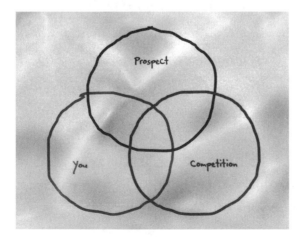

Now ask yourself, how much overlap is there between what you can provide to your prospects and what your competition can provide to your prospects?

If you're like most business-to-business salespeople, you probably said that the overlap is 70 percent or higher. In fact, if you followed a Corporate Visions consultant around the world and listened to the responses we get when we ask that question, the most common answers you would hear would be between 85 and 95 percent overlap.

Regardless of what your exact percentage is, you certainly have overlap with your competition—probably a lot of it.

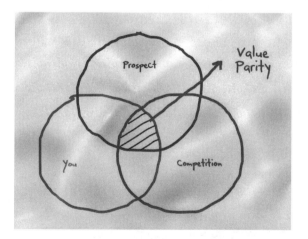

It's our contention that an enormous amount of sales messaging today takes place in the Value Parity area. This is the area where what you have and what the competition has are essentially the same. But when you're looking at the situation this way, where *should* you be focusing your messaging energy and effort?

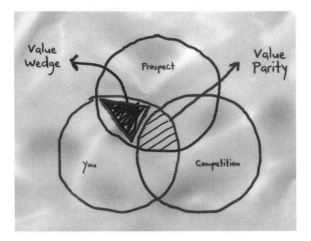

You want to focus it on this area to the left—where what you can do for the customer is different from what the competition can do. This area is called the *Value Wedge*. This is where your best story lives. This is where you find your distinct point of view.

Now, let's take that black triangle and examine it more closely. For something to be in the Value Wedge, it needs to pass three tests.

It needs to be: (1) unique to you; (2) important to the customer; and (3) defensible.

For the rest of this book, when you have something that's unique to you, important to the customer, and defensible, that will be called a *Power Position*.

This is the battleground on which you want to fight. This is what you have to get your prospect to care about. This is where your best story lives.

This is where you will find your distinct point of view.

All right, it's time to find your Power Positions. The Value Wedge diagram will be your guide.

Pick an opportunity that you're working on right now. The idea is to develop some messages that you can use immediately.

The first thing you're going to do is look at your customer. You need to put together a *prospect profile* for this specific opportunity that looks at the key business objectives that the prospect is trying to accomplish. This is your first step in making your message about your customer.

The more specific you can make these business objectives, the better.

For example, when we worked with a company that sold customer relationship management (CRM) solutions, we were first told that one prospect, a vice president of sales, had only one business objective: reaching the revenue target.

While that seems obvious, it's not really true. Vice presidents of sales have more detailed business objectives than just hitting their number. In most companies, they also need to meet the *productivity per rep* target (sales revenue divided by the number of reps they have). They're measured on that constantly, and it drives the way they approach their business. If they can exceed their productivity per rep target, they can usually get permission from the board to hire more sales reps. The opposite is also true.

Another business objective for a vice president of sales is *selling the right mix of products*. A vice president of sales can't just hit her revenue targets by selling legacy products. She also has to make sure that her sales team is getting traction on the products and services that her company is betting its future on. A vice president of sales who can't move those forward-looking solutions will soon be out of a job.

Ideally, you want to find three key business objectives that you can address for your prospect.

(Why three? A lot of memory science shows that remembering one to three things is much easier than remembering four or more. It's the reason that parts of phone numbers and social security numbers are in chunks of three numbers. It's also why most advertising slogans are in threes—think "Snap, Crackle, Pop" or "Absolutely, Positively Overnight.")

That isn't enough, though. You need to dig deeper. If you talk only about a prospect's business objectives, you can end up with an intellectual argument, not a story about your customer. That's not a power message.

So, what are you looking for? You're trying to find things that have a lot of emotional juice for your prospect.

Have you ever heard that people buy on emotion and justify it with facts? It's true. It's true in your personal life, and it's true in your business decisions. Scientists say that it's impossible to make a decision without some emotion to guide you. For those of you who may be skeptical about this, you'll be getting the proof of it later in this book, and you'll hear one of the most remarkable true stories ever told. Again, that's coming later. For now, just know that you are looking for that emotional juice.

How do you know when you've got that juice?

Emotion moves the body. You'll be able to see from people's reactions what really gets them going and what doesn't. When you are faced with a choice between trusting a customer's words or trusting his body language, trust his body language every time.

So what you are looking for in this exercise is that specific juice. If you didn't do discovery with this customer, then for the purposes of this exercise, make your best guess as to what carries the most juice. The best situation, though, is to know because you spoke directly with the customer.

What you want to do now is take the three business objectives that you came up with earlier and identify the top three pains, threats, or challenges that are keeping your prospect from reaching those business objectives. Obviously, they should be pains, threats, or challenges that you can help the prospect solve.

You now have a good sense of your customer's world. It's time to continue around the Value Wedge to your world.

What you're going to do is look at all the things about your offering that you could claim are different from what the competition has. This will work best if you work with at least one other person who knows your product, services, or company. This is a *brainstorming session*. You want to get as much out on the table as possible. If you're going to do this exercise with other people (which we strongly recommend), you need some rules in order to make it work.

The first rule is that anything that anybody says gets captured on paper. At this stage, no one gets to argue that a particular feature, service, or approach is not a differentiator. The reason you need to take this approach is that the best way to get to a high-quality idea is to have a huge quantity of ideas. Following this one rule will have a huge impact on your message.

When we work with companies, we usually do this exercise on a flip chart. If you ask the participants ahead of time if they have much differentiation, they almost always say no. But when you let people just throw stuff up on the paper without critiquing it, you'll end up with three or four flip charts worth of things that you could claim are different about your offerings.

Now, not all of these are going to be good. But when you have a big volume of stuff, good stuff will naturally emerge.

Once you have created as exhaustive a list as possible, you can now look back at it and start to rank the differentiators and identify those that you feel are most compelling. Don't go further than that. You've got one more thing to do.

As you work your way around the Value Wedge diagram, you'll find that you still need to look at your competition for this opportunity.

If you know exactly who your competition is, great.

If you don't know who your competition for this opportunity is, you need to assume the worst.

You need a message that's going to work for you, not one that you'll have to change on the fly.

Here's how you need to look at your competitors. Put their names at the top of separate sheets of paper. Put a line down the middle of each sheet. On the left side of the paper, write the word *strengths*. On the right side of the paper, write the word *weaknesses*. Then, you need to make a list of your competitors' top strengths and weaknesses.

The reasons to list the competitors' weaknesses are obvious enough, but why look at their strengths?

The reason is that sometimes you can turn what looks at first like a competitor's strength into a weakness. And when you do that, it's devastating to your competition.

A great example of this occurred in a recent U.S. presidential contest. By the way, politics is a great place to see messaging at work.

In 2004, the Democrats needed to nominate a candidate to run against President Bush during his reelection campaign. At the time, if you looked at national polls, you saw that the Democrats were viewed as being soft on national security issues. This was a big deal. The United States was at war in Iraq and Afghanistan, and the 9/11 tragedy was still fresh in the nation's mind.

To counteract their perceived weakness on national security issues, the Democrats nominated Senator John Kerry. Kerry had served two tours of duty in Vietnam. He was decorated with a Silver Star, a Bronze Star with Combat V, and three Purple Hearts.

During the Democratic National Convention in Boston, virtually every person who got up on the stage was a former member of the military. Each one extolled Kerry's virtues as a leader who could handle this challenging time in American history. When Kerry was called to the stage to give his acceptance speech, he saluted the audience, and the first words he said were, "I'm John Kerry, and I'm reporting for duty." Many Democrats believed that Kerry's military service was such a strength that there was no way he could be attacked on national security issues.

And yet, he was.

There were the Swift Boat Veterans for Truth and other efforts to call into question his ability to lead the nation through those times. His biggest perceived strength—his military career—was turned into a weak spot. It became a place that he had to defend, as opposed to an area of strength that he could use to attack President Bush.

The point here isn't to take sides on a presidential election from years past. Politics is a rough business, and all of the participants know it. The point is that sometimes you can take what, at first glance, looks like a strength of your competition and turn it into a perceived weakness.

In a recent workshop with a multifunction printer and copier company, this strengths and weaknesses exercise came to a screeching halt. There was a sudden realization that the "box" that actually does the printing and copying didn't have anything that was particularly unique or different from what the competition could offer. In fact, at this company, most of the product managers' time was spent making sure that they had the *same* functionality as the competition, so that they couldn't get beaten by missing a feature here or there.

Then one really bright person in the room offered the idea that the customers' biggest pain point wasn't copying reliability, because all copiers provided basically the same level of service. Instead, the biggest pain point in many facilities was related to the centralization of printing, moving it away from separate office or cube printers to printing centers spread out around the company. This was creating a huge bottleneck.

She then pointed out that some of the new print drivers contained in the company's new software release had advanced scheduling, routing, prioritizing, and alerting capabilities that virtually eliminated the problems that cause bottlenecks in centralized printing environments.

There it was . . . the Value Wedge that the group was looking for. It had nothing to do with the traditional "box" that everyone thinks of when it comes to selling printers and copiers. But it had everything to do with a real customer objective and pain point.

The moral of that story is that you might have to think outside the box to find your Value Wedge. (Groan.)

Okay, you've just gone through the hard work part of this process. Before moving ahead, make sure that you've squeezed all the juice you can out of these exercises. Don't rush them. They're the foundation for everything that comes next.

In this chapter, you've defined the battleground on which you need to fight. You've started creating a story that's about your prospect and that leads to your distinct point of view—those places where you can solve your prospect's problems in a unique way.

In the next chapter, you'll learn the process of simplifying this message further, so that you can tell your story in a way that's simple, differentiated, and memorable—in as little as 30 seconds.

CHAPTER 6

Building Your Story: Power Positions

When Erik's son Zack was eight years old, he told Erik how much he liked books about a kid detective named Jigsaw Jones. Zack said, "Jigsaw Jones says that solving cases is like doing a puzzle; you've got to get all of the clues on the table and then see which ones fit together."

He paused for a minute and then said, "But I think it's even more like a puzzle than that. Grandma taught me that when you're trying to put together a puzzle, you need to look for the edge pieces first; then it all gets easier. I think figuring out a case is like that. You need to find the edge pieces first." It was a pretty smart connection for an eight year old to make.

That same connection is one you need to make in your message. Now that you've got all the pieces of your message on the table, the next thing you're going to do is find your edge pieces, the three key areas that you want to build your message around. Once you find those, the rest of your message gets easier.

You do that through a process called *triangulation*.

Triangulation

1. Find a prospect's pain, threat, or challenge.
2. Match it to a competitor's weakness or vulnerability.
3. Match that to your differentiator as well (or to a group of differentiators).
4. Create a phrase that captures what your prospect will be able to do differently with this solution.

Of the four steps, the last one is where you need guidance.

As you think about this phrase, it's important to think about where it should live on the Message Pyramid.

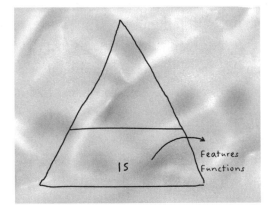

The *Message Pyramid* is a useful way of thinking about the various types of information you need to provide to your customer. You need to tell your customer what your solution Is, what it Does, and what it Means. An example will help make it clear.

When Tylenol first came on the market, it had an ingredient in it that no other medicine was allowed to have—acetaminophen. Acetaminophen is the *Is* of Tylenol. There are other things that go into the pill to hold it together, but the part that does the work, what you're really buying, is the acetaminophen.

Now, what does Tylenol do for you?

Most people's first reaction is to say that Tylenol relieves your pain—which is true. But at the time Tylenol came on the market, there were already other pain relievers out there. And Tylenol would not have become the number one pain reliever in the United States if it had just done the same thing as every other pain reliever.

There was something that Tylenol did that was different. Tylenol didn't just relieve pain. It relieved pain *without upsetting your stomach*.

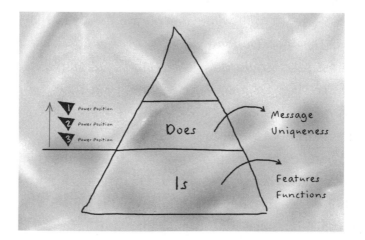

And that's what you can *Do* with Tylenol: you can relieve your pain without upsetting your stomach.

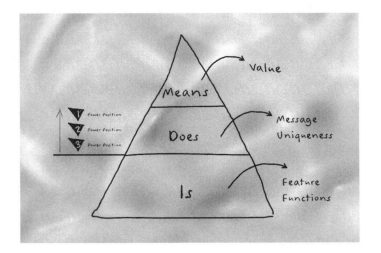

So, what does it *Mean* to use Tylenol? It means that you can be more productive at work, because you don't have either a headache or a stomachache. It means that you can be more patient with your kids, because you're pain-free.

So, what does this have to do with this phrase you're trying to create? You want your phrase to live in the Does layer of the Message Pyramid.

Most salespeople do a good job of talking about the details of their solution—the Is layer. And they also do a pretty good job of talking about the high-level value of their solution—the Means layer.

Where most sales pros drop the ball is in explaining what the customer will be able to Do differently with their solution versus anyone else's. When you can master that, you give yourself a huge advantage against your competition.

This isn't easy, by the way. A few years ago, *60 Minutes* did a story on a company named Razorfish. Razorfish was one of those companies that had a huge run-up in stock value during the Internet bubble. Read this transcript and ask yourself how they did.

60 MINUTES REPORTER: What you do is . . .

RAZORFISH EXECUTIVE: We've recontextualized what it means to be a services business.

60 MINUTES REPORTER: There are people, such as myself, who have trouble with the word *recontextualize*. Tell me what you do. In English.

RAZORFISH EXECUTIVE: We provide services to companies to help them win.

60 MINUTES REPORTER: So do trucking firms . . .

RAZORFISH EXECUTIVE: (interrupting) Absolutely. Absolutely. Absolutely.

60 MINUTES REPORTER: What is it you do?

RAZORFISH EXECUTIVE: Our talent is to do a certain thing, whereas a trucking firm . . .

60 MINUTES REPORTER: (interrupting back) But what is it you do?

RAZORFISH EXECUTIVE: We radically transform businesses to invent and reinvent them.

60 MINUTES REPORTER: That's still very vague.

SECOND RAZORFISH EXECUTIVE: Business strategy.

(Cut to scenes of people working at the office.)

60 MINUTES REPORTER: Translation? Teaching established companies how to make more money and reach out to more customers through the Internet. Or something like that.

They didn't exactly nail it, did they?

Another filter you need to look at is the words that you use in that Does statement. Think of it this way. Imagine that your customer has decided that they have a problem that needs solving, so they bring in you and your top two competitors.

What words and phrases do you think your competitors will use to describe their products and services? We'll get you started. How about

- Flexible
- Customer-focused
- World-class
- Subject matter experts
- Best of breed
- Best in class
- Best ROI
- Easy to use
- Market-leading
- Service-oriented architecture
- Scalable
- Extensible

- Secure
- Robust
- End-to-end
- Comprehensive
- Complete
- Total solution

Now ask yourself what words and phrases you use when you get in front of a prospect. Are they the same as the ones that everyone else uses?

No wonder prospects can't decide which of you they should use. Everyone sounds the same.

You need to separate yourself from your competition. And part of the way you do that is through the words you use.

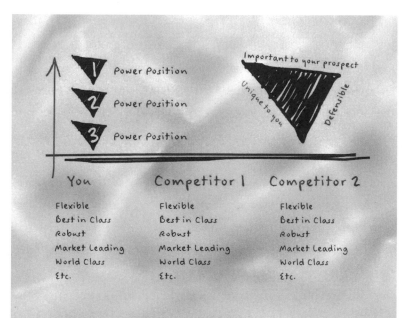

Best Friend Voice

Often companies try to separate themselves by taking the bulleted words just listed and putting the word *really* in front of them.

But we're *really* flexible. We're *really* scalable. We're *really* best in class.

However, do you think your competitors are coming in before you and saying, "You know what's different about us? We're totally inflexible."

Obviously they're not doing that. You need to separate yourself by looking at the words you use in that Does-level statement.

The trick is to use the same words you would use if you were talking to someone you liked.

If a friend asked you how you liked your new car, you probably wouldn't say, "It's great. It completely optimizes my ability to get my family resources from point A to destination B."

You've probably never said to your spouse, "Honey, I feel like we're not fully exploiting the opportunities in our backyard. It's an underutilized resource that's being used at only half of its capacity."

At least, we hope you haven't said any of those things.

And why don't you say those things? Because that's not how you talk to people you like.

So, why would you talk to your customers as if they are people that you *don't* like?

When you create that Does-level statement, use the words that you use when you're talking to friends. Don't use buzzwords or marketing-speak.

When you have those Does-level phrases, you now have the ability *to tell your story short* and *to tell your story long.*

Being able to tell your story short separates the best sales reps from everyone else. Anybody can deliver his message if you give him enough time. It takes true gifts to tell it short.

Mark Twain probably said it best when he wrote, at the end of a long letter to a friend, "I apologize this letter was so long. I didn't have time to write a short one."

It takes work to tell your story short. It doesn't come easily. But it's worth it to learn how to tell your story short. When you can deliver your message in a few seconds, you've got true mastery over your story.

A little while back, Erik was delivering Power Messaging to a client's new-hire class. It was a two-day session out of a much broader two-week training for new hires that the client put all its salespeople through. While he was in the middle of teaching a concept, the chief learning officer (CLO) for the client company walked into the room, interrupted Erik, and said, "I need to speak with you right away."

Erik, having just restarted the class after a break, said that he could talk to her in about 30 minutes.

"It can't wait that long," the CLO said. "I need to talk to you now."

After telling the class that he'd be back as soon as he could, Erik stepped into the hallway and asked the CLO what she needed.

She said she'd just learned that her CEO wanted to have dinner with her that night, and he wanted to know what each third-party vendor was doing for the new-hire training that justified its costs. The CLO was willing to give

Erik until the end of the day to come up with the answer, and she would give the new hires something else to do during that time. It was about 2 p.m.

Erik said that wouldn't be necessary; he could tell her right now what they were getting out of the training. The CLO said, "I don't want just anything. I want your best answer. And it needs to be a paragraph or less. But you've got to get it to me by 5 p.m."

Erik said, "Well, here it is.

"1. Your new hires are learning how to simplify their complex message without dumbing it down or robbing it of its power.

"2. They're learning how to differentiate themselves from the competition in such a way that customers will actually care about that differentiation, so that at the end of their sales cycles, the conversation isn't just about how far they can come down on price.

"3. And finally, they're learning how to deliver their message in a way that is so memorable that even if the prospect doesn't make a buying decision for a week or a month or a year after meeting with them, he'll still remember why he needs to choose them."

The CLO said, "That's great! Can you say it again? I need to write it down."

Erik waited until she got a pen and paper and then repeated it for her. Then, before heading back into the class, he asked, "Why did you think I was going to need until the end of the day to answer your question?"

The CLO said, "Since I knew you were running a class, I called all the other vendors who help us with new-hire training to get their answers first. And they all asked if they could have until tomorrow to get back to me."

Erik was practicing what this book preaches (he'd better be doing that), using the Does-level statements that supported our Power Positions. That made it easy for him to tell his story short. The other guys? They were looking to buy time, starting a fire drill to get something clear, simple, and powerful.

Example: Geico

A lot of people enjoy the Geico gecko commercials. They're fun, and they get your attention. And yet, they still get one of the company's core Power Positions across in a 30-second commercial: "Fifteen minutes can save you 15 percent or more on your car insurance." It's perfect. Simple, specific, and provoking.

You've probably seen one version of the company's commercial in which the big boss has some big ideas for new slogans to promote the company. As we watched this, we couldn't help thinking of the many tagline and elevator pitch exercises we've seen over the years.

A lot of time, expense, and agency hocus-pocus go into creating brand promises, slogans, and taglines. And, here's the amazing irony: most of these statements say absolutely nothing, but at the same time they manage to say the same thing as everyone else.

But Geico serves as a great example of the concepts you've been learning about—Finding your Value Wedge and turning that into a Does-level statement for a Power Position.

If you take a closer look at the Geico statement, it completely nails the prospect's pain points, while showcasing the company's uniqueness:

- *Fifteen minutes.* Hey, people don't have a lot of time, and they don't want to make the effort to meet with insurance agents. Tim had an insurance agent friend who just retired, saying that he was glad he was getting out of the business, as the Internet was taking over. He said, "People aren't going to want to have a relationship with their insurance agent anymore." Tim replied, "I hate to break it to you, friend, but people never wanted to have a relationship with their insurance agent."
- *Save 15 percent or more.* Everyone knows that insurance is a necessary evil. No one wants to pay more for it than she has to. The thought that your insurance carrier is overcharging you is always at the back of your mind. Car insurance is a blatant commodity. Why overpay a middleman for adding no value to the transaction? If you can make it easy to see that someone is ripping you off, and then make it painless to make a change, you have a Value Wedge against the competition.

What Can the Prospect Do Better or Differently?

The other thing that the Geico messaging does right is that it focuses on what the customer can do better, or at least differently, as a result of your solution—the Does-level statement. It doesn't talk about the insurance, what it is, or even what it does. It talks about what you can do as a result.

We know what you are thinking. It's easy to create a clear, powerful slogan when you are the low-price leader. Wal-Mart doesn't require much imagination in its marketing, right?

The same principles apply when you are trying to maintain your prices and protect your margins, even though your buyers are trying to force you into a commodity trap.

Imagine that your job is to sell commercial cleaning services. Things don't get much more commoditized than that. How would you find your Power Positions? How would you find your distinct point of view?

We worked with a commercial cleaning company that wanted to convince the owners of multitenant office buildings to choose its cleaning service over all of the other national and local options.

The company found one of their Power Positions by tapping into the issue of staff health and absenteeism. It approached building owners and showed them how it could help them market their office space by promoting their choice in a cleaning company.

How? By focusing the decision on which cleaning service did the best job at "cleaning for health," not just cleaning the surfaces in the space. Its Does-level Power Position statement was, "Get a healthier clean at no extra cost." The landlords used it as a way to differentiate themselves when competing against other landlords offering office space. They explained to potential renters how their cleaning service uses unique, proven approaches to disinfecting and avoiding cross-contamination to improve building and staff health.

Of course, the cleaning company did a lot of different things and offered a bunch of cleaning services. But it was able to ride its Power Position to increase its deal size and close rates.

When you have completed the exercises in this chapter, you will have the bones of the Power Position–based story that you're trying to tell. You'll also have the foundation from which you are going to provoke your customer and share your distinct point of view.

Next, you are going to look at how you can get prospects to care about what's different about you. To do that, you need to deliver this message in a different way.

All sales coaching tells you to make your message be about your prospect. Yet, they never really tell you how to do that. In the next chapter, you'll learn how to make sure that this story is about your customer, as opposed to being a story about you.

CHAPTER 7

You Phrasing: Creating Engagement and Ownership

At the time this book was being written, if you were to look at the outside of a Starbucks cup, you'd see the word *you* in a giant font. If you read the next few lines, you'd see this:

> You've been working with Conservation International for 10 years. . . . (explains how) . . . It makes a difference. Just like you do. Congratulations, you.

On the brown cardboard sleeve that keeps the cup from feeling too warm in your hand, you'd also read:

> Learn more about other ways you're helping make a difference at . . . (gives URL).

Why does Starbucks say that "you" did all these things? You just bought a cup of coffee, right? Its people are the ones who worked with Conservation International.

Starbucks put its message together this way because it understands the immense power of one little word.

This chapter is about a simple, but profound concept called *you phrasing*.

As you continue to build out your story—the message that you need to tell your customer—you need to make sure that your customer remains at the center of this story. You phrasing helps you do that.

You phrasing transfers ownership to your listener. That's what you see Starbucks doing with the message that it puts on its cups. You become the focus of the story being told, not them.

You phrasing helps you sell in another way. When you use you phrasing, your prospect's unconscious mind tries out your solution as you describe what he can do with it. He is no longer a passive listener. He is actively engaging your ideas.

You phrasing pulls your prospect into the story you are telling. And once that happens, you get a measurable impact.

In a study published in 1982, the power of you phrasing was put to the test. In Tempe, Arizona, researchers went door to door saying that they were conducting a survey to test attitudes toward cable television. Cable was very new at the time.

The objective of the experiment was to test the difference between telling someone about a service and getting them to imagine what it would be like to use the new service. So, some people were given this information (the following is a portion of the script):

> CATV will provide a broader entertainment and informational service to its subscribers. Used properly, a person can plan in advance to enjoy events offered. Instead of spending money on the babysitter and gas, and putting up with the

hassles of "going out," more time can be spent at home with family, alone, or with friends.

The same information was conveyed to a separate set of people using you phrasing to cause them to imagine what it would be like to use the new service. Here's a portion of that script:

> Take a moment and imagine how CATV will provide *you* with a broader entertainment and informational service. When *you* use it properly, *you* will be able to plan in advance which of the events offered *you* wish to enjoy. Take a moment and think of how, instead of spending money on the babysitter and gas, and then having to put up with the hassles of "going out," *you* will be able to spend *your* time at home, with *your* family, alone, or with *your* friends.

As you can see, the difference between the two scripts was very subtle.

So, what were the results? Did you phrasing have an impact on sales?

Over the next six weeks, all of the subjects were contacted by company salespeople (who weren't told of the experiment) as part of CATV's standard door-to-door marketing. All of the subjects were offered the opportunity to have a free week of service or the opportunity to subscribe to the service. The results were impressive.

People who had heard the you-phrasing description of the service accepted the free week 66 percent of the time, whereas the control group took the free week of service offer only 42 percent of the time.

The impact on people who were willing to *buy* the service was even more impressive. Those who heard the you-phrasing description of the service subscribed 47 percent of the time, not even waiting to try the free week. The control group subscribed only 20 percent of the time.

The simple use of one small word, *you*, had doubled the number of sales in this experiment.

Many sales training courses teach you to use *we phrasing*—use *we* and not *you* in your message. But, *we* can mean "we, the vendor" or "we, you plus us." Either way, it subconsciously gives your customer permission to keep her distance, sit back, and disengage from your message.

Here are a couple of examples of what you don't want to do.

"When I want to insert a picture into Microsoft Word, first I click the Insert tab, then I click on Picture, then I browse for the file that I want to add, and finally, I click the Insert button."

That is *I phrasing*.

A lot of people would rather say: "When we want to insert a picture into Microsoft Word, first we click the Insert tab, then we click on Picture, then we browse for the file that we want to add, and finally, we click the Insert button."

Who is we? Me, you, or us? A bit confusing, isn't it? When people say *we*, it's often just a different form of I phrasing.

Another thing that's strange about we phrasing is that you don't use it when you're talking to people you like.

Outside of selling, people don't use we phrasing much at all. One of the few exceptions occurs when adults are talking to children. Sometimes you'll hear adults say, "So, Jimmy, how are we doing today?"

But, do you really want to treat your customer like a child?

The other time you might hear people use we phrasing is in a hospital. If you've ever been in a hospital bed and had a nurse or doctor walk into your room, at some point you've heard him say, "So, how are we doing today?" And if you've ever been the one lying in that bed, you've probably felt like saying, "I don't know how *we* are doing today, but *I'm* in a hospital bed. Maybe you could up my meds a bit."

An example of the effective use of you phrasing happens at the end of every jury trial. You see the prosecutor standing in front of the jury making her final summation. What you never hear her say is, "Over the last two weeks, based on what I've seen with my own eyes and what I've heard with my own ears—this person is guilty." You never hear her say that.

You also never hear her say, "Based on what we've seen with our own eyes and what we've heard with our own ears, this person is guilty."

What you do hear her say is, "Based on what *you've* seen with *your* own eyes and what *you've* heard with *your* own ears, this person is guilty."

She's transferring ownership at the unconscious level. It's a powerful way to message.

This may seem pretty subtle to you. Perhaps it seems unimportant. But you phrasing isn't just a technique. It's a mind-set. It forces you into your customer's world.

It's reminiscent of how Benjamin Zander, conductor of the Boston Philharmonic, talks about music. As he's addressing an audience, he'll start playing the piano. As the music builds, he starts playing furiously. And then, he'll stop, freezing in the position that he's in at that moment. He'll be rocked to one side, his face filled with emotion and his hands above the keyboard. And he'll tell the audience:

"Do you see what happened to my body? The music pushed me here."

He calls it "one-buttock" playing. His body moves the way the music commands it to.

You phrasing has a similar effect. Once you start you phrasing, you'll find yourself pulled into your prospect's world more deeply than you ever were before. You can't help it. You phrasing pushes you there. And that helps you connect your story to your customer's story in a deep and powerful way. So while it can seem like just an interesting technique, its power accumulates over time.

You need to practice you phrasing. If you're like most sales professionals, you've got grooves in your manner of speaking that make you use we phrasing for almost everything. Start by instructing someone else to do something. Here's a simple example:

"When *you* want to insert a picture into Microsoft Word, first *you* click the Insert tab, then *you* click on Picture, then *you* browse for the file that *you* want to add, and finally, *you* click the Insert button."

Now who is taking ownership? Me or you? When you use you phrasing, you are helping your prospect's unconscious mind feel like it's participating.

We diffuses the focus. *You* makes the prospect try your product or service. Begin replacing the word *we* or *I* with the word *you* in your selling conversations.

Here is a list of common phrases that need you phrasing. Move away from saying things like:

"What I'm going to show you . . ."
"Our company allows you to . . ."
"The system allows you to . . ."
"Next, I'm going to . . . "
"We need to be able to . . . "
"What if I could show you . . . "

Notice the subtle but powerful change when you switch to you phrasing:

"What *you'll* see . . . "
"What *you'll* be able to do is . . . "
"Next, *you'll* be able to . . . "
"*You* need to be able to . . . "
"What if *you* could . . . "

Switching to you phrasing makes a huge difference with your audience. It's a simple change with enormous results. Now, you'll listen to an actual example.

You Phrasing for Toilet Cleaning

As you read in the previous chapter, a national franchise commercial cleaning business came to us recently. Its goal was to get out of the brutal price wars. Deal sizes also were eroding.

One of the cleaning company's top market segments is medical facilities. When their Inside Sales Team called on managers, the most popular sales introduction used by the company's salespeople was

> Hi, I'm Mary from ACME cleaning. We are a 25-year-old cleaning company with 1,500 locations. We are cleaning more than 8,000 medical facilities and clinics like yours. We'd like to stop in to measure your facility and give you an instant, no obligation quote. Would you like to see if we can do better than your current cleaning service?

What was happening? Salespeople were burning a lot of energy going out to provide free quotes for prospects that weren't in a buying cycle. Salespeople were fabricating a sales cycle by forcing an event. However, proposal close rates were dropping fast as a result of this unqualified and undifferentiated approach.

Once the sales rep was onsite, the we phrasing continued.

> We use the latest in microfiber technology in our cloths and mops, which has been shown to clean bacteria three times better than cotton cloths and string mops. We have a partnership with Procter & Gamble–branded products to use the latest in cleaning supplies. We also have a unique training program and a multicolor cloth system that helps significantly reduce the risk of cross-contamination.

As you can see, this is a laundry list of features and benefits that have no context and no relevance to the buyer. Nothing asks him to contrast the solution that is being offered to his current situation or asks him to take ownership of the problem and the solution.

Now, listen to how the story changes when you phrasing is applied, along with several other concepts that you've already learned in this book.

Imagine that you are the facilities manager at a medical office, clinic, or outpatient center, and you have just picked up the phone. It's ACME Cleaning Services on the other end. And this is what you hear. (*Note:* You'll see the salesperson's name and the word *we* in the first 10 words here. What's important is how quickly the focus changes to *you.*)

> Hi, this is Mary from ACME Cleaning. We are asking medical facilities managers like *you* how you feel *your* after-hours cleaning service is contributing—positively or negatively—to *your* patient safety and staff health objectives.

That's a big change. Instead of talking about who the company is and what it does, the conversation is immediately addressed to the buyer, the buyer's objectives, and his emotional investment in making the right decisions that affect those objectives. You've now successfully increased the strategic altitude of your message. Now, listen to the follow-up statement from the salesperson, which has been prepared in advance to move the dialogue forward in a desired direction, regardless of the response:

> *You* may have heard that there's a recent ABC study that indicates that of the infections caught inside medical facilities, one-third are due to improper cleaning techniques.
>
> How well do *you* feel your after-hours cleaning providers have been trained and certified on proper disinfecting and avoiding cross-contamination?

Instead of jumping into products and features, this seller is creating even more engagement using you phrasing. The buyer has to reckon with this startling, real-world statistic, especially when it is attached to a provocative you-phrased question.

On the first call, the buyer could easily delegate the dialogue to a lower-level purchasing staffer. But now the conversation has been squarely linked to the buyer's objectives, and he is actively engaged in considering the consequences of the cleaning service decision.

> What if *you* could leave work each night knowing that *your* after-hours cleaning service is using the right processes and tools to improve disinfecting and eliminate cross-contamination?

"What if you . . ." questions are a simple, effective you-phrasing technique. Now who owns solving the problem? Me or you? When you use you phrasing, you are helping your prospect's unconscious mind feel as if it's already participating in the solution.

Now you are finally ready to talk about what you do. But don't forget your you phrasing:

> Imagine the impact on *your* safety and health objectives if *your* after-hours cleaning service were . . .
>
> Using microfiber cloths and mops, instead of cotton, to improve *your* disinfecting by eliminating 99 percent of bacteria rather than using traditional approaches that get rid of only 30 percent.
>
> Using multicolored cloths to ensure that it isn't using the same cloth in *your* bathrooms that it uses to clean *your* office phones.

How could a system like this help ensure that *your* cleaners do everything in their power to avoid cross-contamination?

Deal Size Increases 21 percent

The impact of changing the dialogue drove an increase in deal size of 21 percent.

Nothing else changed. The company didn't acquire or develop new products. Its salespeople simply changed the conversation so that it was about the prospect and what she cared about. They applied you phrasing.

There is one challenge to be aware of when using you phrasing. You phrasing is powerful because it transfers ownership at the unconscious level. You need to make it a part of the way you convey your message every day. Just like any powerful tool, if you use it poorly, it could cause you some problems.

In particular, what you don't want to do with you phrasing is *transfer blame* to your customers.

And you never will do that when you apply the next chapter's filter as you create your story.

CHAPTER 8

The Hero Model: Play the Right Part

What do *The Matrix, Star Wars,* the *Harry Potter* books, and the best sales messages all have in common? They all follow the same storytelling model.

Joseph Campbell had a great job. He was a mythologist. He traveled to more than 100 countries documenting myths and hero stories. What he found was both insightful and applicable to field messaging: across boundaries of geography, culture, and language, all these hero stories follow a similar pattern. What he learned inspired him to write a book entitled *The Hero with a Thousand Faces.*

His book is required reading if you want to become a screenwriter, film director, or movie producer. George Lucas went back and reread Campbell's book when he was developing a cohesive story for *Star Wars.*

Campbell called this storytelling model the "Mono-Myth" (meaning the One Story) because all the hero stories he found told this same story over and over again, even though the setting and the names might change.

Here's what this means to you: If you want to produce a movie that will sell millions of dollars worth of box office tickets, you will use this hero model to tell your story. If you want to sell millions of dollars worth of your solution, you will use this same model to tell your story.

The model is a simple one. It has five basic steps:

Step 1. The world is normal.

Step 2. Something changes.

Step 3. The hero pushes back.

Step 4. Enter the mentor.

Step 5. The hero saves the day.

Now, let's go a little deeper.

Step 1. The model starts out with everything being normal. Remember when you first see Luke Skywalker in the first *Star Wars* movie? He's not doing anything special. He is helping his uncle farm the land where they live. And he's bored. Until . . .

Step 2. Something changes. In *Star Wars*, Luke meets the droids, R2D2 and C3PO, and gets the message from Princess Leia. Later, he discovers that his uncle's farm has been attacked, both his aunt and uncle have been killed, and the farm has been destroyed. And then he's asked to fight back, but what does he do?

Step 3. The hero resists the call to action. At first, Luke doesn't think that there's any way he can fight back. The odds seem too great. And then . . .

Step 4. The mentor enters the picture. In *Star Wars*, the mentor is Obi Wan Kenobi. He helps Luke believe that he can fight back, and that he must assume his rightful position as the hero. And then . . .

Step 5. The hero saves the day. At the end of *Star Wars*, it's not Obi Wan who defeats the Death Star. It's Luke.

This same model is repeated in virtually every hero story. Sometimes, it's subtle. For example, if you're familiar with the Spiderman story, you might think that he didn't have a mentor. But when you look a little more closely, you see that he did. His Uncle Ben was mentoring him when he said, "With great power comes great responsibility."

And the takeaway for you is that there is a reason why all these hero stories are told the same way. There's something in the brain that responds favorably to this model, no matter what the culture. You need to harness the power of this model as you create your customer story.

The reason that this hero model is so effective in moviemaking is that as human beings, we live our lives in this hero model. Haven't there been times in your life when something changed that caused you to make decisions about the direction your life would take?

What's different between you and your heroes is that your reluctance often overpowers the call to adventure. Your fear of the unknown holds you back from discovering a new world. Yet, there have been times in your life when a parent or teacher or coach or manager encouraged you to go beyond what you believed you were capable of.

All of this hero-story talk leads up to this question: in a typical sales conversation, what role does the sales rep assume? The hero, right?

You ride in on your white horse saying,

We can save the day!
We can lower your cost.
We can save you money.
Our solutions allow you to . . .
We helped ABC Company maximize its productivity.

You're the hero in this story. And that should not be your role, should it?

Whose role should it be?

Of course—it's your customers' role. They are the ones that need to save the day—not you.

What is your role? That of the mentor.

You are there to help your customers see what has changed in their world and how they, by accepting their call, can adapt and better survive and thrive.

You need to turn your customers into heroes.

So, what does messaging that makes your customer the hero, instead of you and your company, look like?

Look at what you've constructed so far when you created your Power Positions. You put together a message that looked at your customers' world today—their business objectives and their pains. Then you looked at how they can solve those problems with your solution.

In a real-world sales interaction, you should expect the customer to push back at this point. He might say, "It'll take too much time, too much money. I'm really not in that much trouble." That's when you show him how much value he can get from your solution. And you help him see that you can be a mentor for him through your Proof points, because you bring knowledge to the table that he didn't have. (You'll get a whole chapter devoted to Proof points later in the book.)

You don't just let your customers sit where they are, convinced that they can't make changes. You have the tools to challenge them and encourage them to make the changes they need to make.

And at the end of the day, you're going to use you phrasing (from the last chapter) to show your customer that he is the hero, as opposed to I phrasing or we phrasing, which would make you the hero of this story.

As you create this story using the tools you've seen so far, here are some additional tips for making the prospect the hero of your story.

First, decide who is going to be the villain. Every hero story needs a villain. Unfortunately, if you don't pick a villain, and if you use you phrasing incorrectly, sometimes the prospect sounds like the villain.

You have outdated processes.
You haven't kept up with the competition.
Your people haven't adjusted to the changing times.

That's not the way to use you phrasing. You phrasing is powerful because it transfers ownership at the unconscious level. But you don't want to transfer ownership of blame. That doesn't do you any good.

And yet, this piece still needs a villain. So, who or what should be the villain in your story?

If you said some outside force, then you nailed it. The villain is not the prospect's systems or its people. The villain is something that's changed in the environment.

It could be new government regulations. It could be new market conditions. It could be changes in competition or technology.

Your story needs to let your prospect know that back when she made the decision to buy the solution that she already has in place, it was the best decision she could possibly have made.

And it's only because of changes in the environment—changes that are coming now, and fast—that she needs to look at doing something different.

The same thing is true of your prospect's people. To do the hero model well, you should never imply that the prospect's people are anything other than hardworking, high-integrity, conscientious employees. Everybody wants to believe that about his people. And he's right.

Your story needs to be about good people who are trapped by systems or processes that no longer meet the needs of the changing environment.

To give you an example of the power of the hero model to help you even in tricky messaging situations, consider this example.

A client of ours came to us with an interesting problem. He was trying to sell a new software system to two brothers who owned a company together. After doing some discovery, the members of the sales team decided that they could help this company. The prospect's system was holding them back from being as successful a business as they could be.

The challenge was that the person who had designed the existing system was the *mother* of the two brothers who owned the business. Now, how do you tell those two brothers that mom's system needs to be replaced? Enter the hero model.

When they heard the hero model, they knew exactly what to do. Their messaging simply followed the hero model formula. Listen.

> You know, when this system was designed, it was a perfect fit for your environment. Unfortunately, things have changed. Since your system was put together, new government regulations have come out, and the competitive landscape and customer expectations have changed. Today, you need a system that's been designed to take those new realities into account. Your people have worked hard to overcome some of the new challenges, but it's putting a greater burden on them every day. The reason companies are coming to us is that they are looking for a way to succeed in this new environment. And when they can do that, they're able to gain a competitive advantage. As an example, one customer of ours faced exactly these same challenges . . .

You can hear how a focus shift took an uncomfortable situation and turned it into great messaging.

If all you take away from this book is Power Positions, you phrasing, and the hero model, you'll have enough to make a huge impact on your messaging. But this is just the beginning. Now, the fun starts.

In the next chapters, you'll learn approaches that can help make any message more simplified, differentiated, and memorable. You'll learn how to make sure that your message survives after you've left the room.

PART 3

YOUR POWER MESSAGE

CHAPTER 9

The Hammock: Getting Their Attention

I t's a beautiful summer morning on Lake Erie. The sun's out, but there's just enough breeze to keep you comfortable. It's not too hot and not too cold.

Erik's lying in a hammock next to a beach. He's got a book in his hand, and some chips and a drink are on a small table within easy reach. It's a pretty good life.

Erik's five-year-old son Brett doesn't appreciate all the things that had to come together to make this moment happen: scheduling vacation; having a place to go; the weather being perfect; a good book to read.

All Brett knows is that his dad is ignoring him. And Brett wants to play with his dad.

Brett stands beside the hammock and starts talking. He's talking about something fairly random, as five-year-olds so often do.

Erik pretends that he's paying attention. He tries to give Brett yeses and nos in the right places. Every once in a while, Erik gives Brett a "that sounds cool."

It works for a bit, but then Brett realizes that Erik isn't really paying attention to him. Erik's still reading his book.

So, now Brett starts to push on the hammock to make it swing. At first, Erik keeps ignoring him. Erik loves Brett, but he really wants this moment of relaxation. They're going to have a week together, which means that there will be plenty of time for the two of them to play. But there's no guarantee that the weather will be like this again, and no guarantee that there will be this perfect hammock time again.

Brett pushes the hammock harder.

He keeps it up until Erik can't ignore him anymore. Erik looks up from his book, and Brett's got a big grin on his face. He knows he's got Erik's attention now. Erik smiles back at him and gets up from the hammock. And they go play.

The situation that Brett was facing—wanting Erik's full attention and Erik wanting to pretend that Brett had it rather than actually giving it to him—is the same situation that sales professionals face every day.

Your prospect didn't wake up this morning and say, "I hope a salesperson calls me today, stops me from doing what I'd planned, and gets me to do something different." If only the world worked that way!

But that's not how it works. Your prospect has things that she is trying to accomplish. She often isn't looking to make a change. Her focus is on things other than your message.

And even when you feel you have her attention, she's often just faking it.

Getting people's attention is the great challenge facing anybody who is trying to deliver a message today. There is a ridiculous volume of people, ideas, and things, all clamoring for attention to the point that it can be overwhelming.

From your prospects' perspective, you can think of the challenges as being *information* related. There is so much information coming at your prospects every day that they need systems and defenses that help them sort through it all.

From *your* perspective, though, you should think of your challenge as being an *attention* problem. In a world in which there is so much competition for your prospect's attention, how do you stand out? How do you get and earn your prospect's attention?

And your challenge goes still further than that. It's not just initial attention.

Just because your prospect agrees to the first phone call or the first meeting doesn't mean that you're going to have his attention throughout the sales cycle when you deliver your message. In fact, science shows that you may not have his full attention even during that first face-to-face meeting. Just as Brett had to work hard to get his dad's attention, even though he was talking to his dad and standing right next to him, you need to work for every moment of your prospect's attention.

Whether you know it or not, your prospect is in a "hammock" that's just as real as Brett's dad's hammock, even though it's invisible.

What Science Tells You about Messaging

There's neuroscience research that speaks to the challenge that all salespeople face when they are giving a message, no matter how they deliver that message—i.e., in person, over the phone, through the Web, or in any other way.

Researchers gave people a list of words and told them, "You can look at this list of words once, then we're going to take it away, and we want you to write down every word that you're able to remember."

Here is what the researchers found.

They found that people could remember 70 percent of the words at the beginning of the list, 20 percent of the words in the middle of the list, and 100 percent of the words that were at the end of the list.

The fact that the people tested could remember a lot of the words at the end of the list isn't too surprising, is it? Those were the last words they saw; they ought to be able to remember them best.

But if you think about it, it seems logical that you should be able to remember the words in the middle much more easily than the words at the beginning. After all, you heard the beginning words furthest back in time, so those ought to be the hardest words to remember. But that's not the way it works.

Look at the evidence. You're more than three times as likely to remember the information that was at the beginning of that list than the information that was in the middle. Why?

Well, what the researchers have discovered is that at the beginning of anything, your brain is so awake, alive, and alert, and there are so many more neurons firing than there are later on, that you're able to capture information and get impact from information much more effectively.

So, what does that have to do with how you message? Well, look at an example from the traditional opening of a business-to-business sales presentation. You open the meeting with: "Here's our founder, here's our history, this is when we started; here's our company headquarters and our office locations; here are all of the products we've ever developed; and here are the logos of a bunch of our customers."

By the time you're actually ready to talk about the customer's problem and differentiate your product or service as a solution to that problem, where is that information being delivered? Down in the 20-percent zone, where your prospect has tuned out and is not paying attention.

It's much more difficult to get the impact of the power of your product or the power of your message across in the middle of your meeting than it would have been if you'd put the message right up front. Plus, that opening is the same as everyone else's first five slides, so you've completely wasted the moment when a buyer is most engaged in your message.

So this is what you want to change. You want to establish a keen understanding of the customer's business problems, communicate the power of your solution, and demonstrate your uniqueness. And you need to do that at the beginning of your meeting.

And then, when you get to the close, you want to do the same thing. You want to make sure that you've built to a crescendo, orchestrating the biggest impact that you can get with that prospect.

Throughout the rest of this book, this challenge will be referred to as the Hammock. In part, this is because the graph looks like a hammock, and in part, it's because you need to recognize that your challenge is to keep your customer's brain from wandering or going to sleep during your messaging.

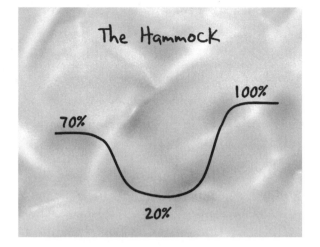

So, how long do you naturally have someone's attention at the beginning of a meeting?

According to John Medina, author of the brilliant book *Brain Rules* and the director of the Brain Center for Applied Learning Research, several peer-reviewed studies show that you naturally have someone's attention for about 10 minutes before that person loses focus on your message. As you can see from the previous graph, those studies also support the visual concept of the Hammock.

You want to take advantage of those first 10 minutes of an in-person meeting to get your message across. But does the Hammock affect other methods that you use to deliver your message?

What about e-mail, for example? Here's the thing to know about e-mail: most people skim through their e-mails, looking for any reason *not* to read them (or to put them in a folder marked *later*—and then never read them).

Obviously, the Hammock is in play here, as well. The first thing you need to understand is that your subject line needs to be interesting enough to get your prospect to open your e-mail. Then, your first sentence needs to be interesting enough to get your prospect to want to read the rest of the e-mail.

A good way to think about this is to look at your e-mails in your e-mail windowpane. That's how most people will see them. They'll see your subject line and probably the first sentence. Then ask yourself, does this material make you want to continue reading? Or does it make you want to put it in a folder to be "read" later? You should also check how your e-mail looks when it's read on a smartphone, since a growing number of e-mails are read that way.

What about Web-based presentations? Do you think the Hammock applies there, too?

Of course it does. In fact, ask yourself this simple question: what were you doing the last time you were on the receiving end of a Web-based presentation? If you're like most people, you were doing anything but paying attention to the message.

So, just assume that you don't have people's attention. What will you do with your message to avoid the Hammock? You need to start your Web meetings in a way that grabs people's attention, and you need to end them in a way that keeps the emotional energy going.

What about over the phone? Does the Hammock apply there? Years ago, Erik was told of a study done by AT&T that showed that, when you are cold calling, you've got 10 seconds to get a prospect's attention from the time she says, "Hello."

To make matters worse, this 10-second clock starts over and over several times in the first couple of minutes of a phone call, with the prospect on the other end making a judgment call about whether or not to continue the call several times. It takes many rounds of successfully gaining agreement before you build enough rapport to get off the 10-second clock.

Unfortunately, we haven't been able to find the original study to support Erik's recollection. However, when you ask a room full of people at our sales training events if it sounds about right, they always say yes. So, it appears that the Hammock is in play on phone calls, as well as everywhere else.

The reality is that every time you deliver your message, no matter what the format (in person with PowerPoint, over the phone, over the Web, sitting across the table, in e-mail, and so on), you have to constantly fight the impact that the Hammock has on your prospect's ability to give you his attention.

Stay Out of the Hammock

So, how do you fight the Hammock? How do you make sure that your message is remembered? To do that, you need to understand a bit of the science around how our brains are wired.

Many years ago, scientists believed that all parts of the brain participated in all of the brain's functions. That meant that if you had damage to 10 percent of your brain, you'd lose 10 percent of your memories, 10 percent of your ability to do math, 10 percent of your ability to read and write, and so on.

Today, scientists know that that's not the way the brain works. In fact, the brain is divided into three primary areas that nest within each other like those Russian ceramic dolls that always seem to contain one more inside.

The outer layer, which is called the *neocortex*, is the wrinkly part of the brain. It sits on top, and humans have the largest neocortex in the animal kingdom. You can think of the neocortex as the brain's computer. It loves to process data, and it will process and process all day long and be happy doing it.

Underneath the neocortex, sitting inside it almost like a ball sits inside a glove, is the *limbic system*. The limbic system is where emotions reside—love, hate, and the varying shades of human feelings.

And underneath the limbic system, sort of like a stick that holds up a Popsicle, are the *brain stem* and other older brain structures. Popular writing calls this section the *reptile brain*. We prefer to use the term given to it by Robert Ornstein, formerly a professor of neurobiology at Stanford University and today chairman of the Institute for the Study of Human Knowledge. Ornstein refers to this section of the brain as the *Old Brain*. The Old Brain cares about survival.

So, what does the Old Brain have to do with the problem of the Hammock? Your Old Brain acts as a filter. It decides what gets noticed—what gets your attention.

If you were to see your prospect's Old Brain at the beginning of a meeting or a phone call, reading an e-mail, or while you were on the Web, you'd see it lit up like a Christmas tree. Why? The prospect's Old Brain needs to do a "fight or flight" assessment. In effect, it is asking, "This information I'm getting right now, how must I react? Will it help me live longer? Will it kill me?"

Now, if you take as an example the start of a typical PowerPoint presentation, when the lights go down and the PowerPoint goes up on the wall, your customer's Old Brain says, "I've seen this before. This won't help me live longer, and this won't kill me. I can go to sleep for a while."

And it stays asleep until it hears the magic words that come at the end of the presentation and spike the Old Brain back up. What are those magic words?

"In conclusion . . ."
"In summary . . ."
"To wrap it up . . ."

The sound of those magic words lifts the Old Brain up out of the Hammock. Why? Because they signal that this event is coming to an end, so the Old Brain needs to be prepared to assess the next thing that's going to possibly affect its survival.

This is the challenge that you face every time you try to deliver your message. And it's not that your prospects are being unprofessional. It's not that your prospects are being rude.

In fact, you've experienced this many times yourself. You've been in meetings where you knew you were getting important information. And you've spaced out for 15 minutes of the meeting. Why? Because of the way your brain works.

Use Grabbers

So, the Hammock is a natural brain pattern. The question is, can you change it?

And the answer is, "Yes, you can. You have to."

Regardless of the form your sales messaging takes, you need to have a "hot opening" and a "hot close," and you need to "spike" your prospect's attention in the middle.

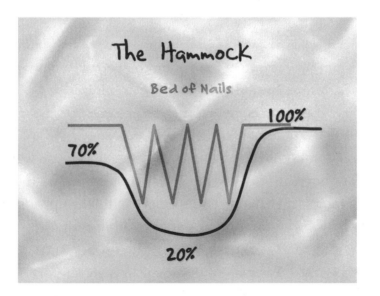

So, how do you create those spikes? You do it by using a technique called *Grabbers*.

Grabbers work because they break the pattern that the Old Brain is expecting when you deliver your message.

In fact, in many ways, the attention formula is a simple one. If you want to bury your prospect in the Hammock, simply deliver your message exactly the same way everyone else does. You'll guarantee that your message is forgotten, or at least confused with your competitors' messages.

You've experienced this before if you've ever been in a sales cycle where your prospect is meeting with you and also meeting with your competition.

Think of it this way. Have you ever been going along in that competitive sales cycle—maybe it's your second, third, or fourth meeting—and had a prospect say to you, "Now, remind me again, are you the folks who solve this problem (fill-in-blank) way? Or are you the guys who solve it (fill-in-blank) way?"

Why don't prospects remember how your solution works and how it differs from your competitors' solutions? Because you delivered your message in almost the exact same way as your competitors, this causes a problem in memory that psychologists call *interference*.

Interference is the problem that occurs when you learn similar things in similar ways. It becomes very hard for your brain to find the precise memory that corresponds to that event. It gets jumbled up with similar memories.

It's the same reason why, if you travel a lot, you've had this experience. You park your car at your home airport. You get on a plane for a business trip. You return to your home airport sometime later. And if you haven't written down the number of your parking space, can you find your car? Nope.

Why not? You parked there not that long ago.

The explanation is interference. You see, if you travel frequently, you've parked at that airport many, many times. And what happens is, your mind can no longer keep your most recent parking spot separate from all of the others.

Again for frequent travelers, the same thing is true if you've ever gone to a city, rented a car, parked at your hotel at night, and then walked out into the parking lot the next morning and wondered, "What the heck did I drive here last night?" Even though you just parked there the night before, it's still hard to remember what you drove, because you've had similar experiences so many times previously.

The metaphor that psychologists use to describe this is that your brain is like a bucket full of white marbles. Think of the next memory you add to that bucket as being a white pearl. Once that white pearl gets dropped into that bucket of white marbles and swirled around, how hard is it going to be to find that white pearl? Pretty hard.

If you want memories to stick and to be easily retrieved by your prospect, you need to have your message create a memory that's so different that it's like a black pearl placed into that bucket of white marbles. No matter how much that bucket gets swirled around, it's always going to be easy to find that black pearl.

The way to create that black pearl memory is to break the pattern that the Old Brain expects. The way to create that black pearl memory is to do something different.

That's what Grabbers are all about. They give you a way to break the pattern. They create spikes of attention during your messaging.

You can think of those spikes as being like a "bed of nails." It's really hard to fall asleep when you're lying on a bed of nails, as opposed to lazily rocking in a hammock.

Now, what should all of these spikes support? Your Power Positions (Chapter 6). That's the part of your message that you want to get to stick. That's what you want your prospect to remember.

Next, you'll learn how to use Grabbers to create the hot opening, the hot close, and the attention spikes along the way.

CHAPTER 10

Grabbers: Creating Impact

As you deliver your message, you will use Grabbers to create your hot openings, hot closes, and spikes in the middle of your message. *Grabbers* get your prospect emotionally involved, literally and figuratively leaning into your message. Grabbers are the "wow" of your message.

Once you have your prospects leaning into your message, you need to show them the "how" part of your message. The technique you'll use to do that will be covered in a later chapter. You'll also need to prove your claims. Proof will be discussed later in this book, as well.

Wow, how, and proof are the three messaging components you'll need for each of your Power Positions. Don't worry. Your message won't feel redundant or formulaic to the prospect. You've got a ton of options to choose from. What it will do is keep your prospect out of the Hammock and make him hear a simple, differentiated, and memorable message.

Here are four types of Grabber techniques to create the "wow" in your message:

- What-if-you questions
- Number plays
- Customer stories with contrast
- 3D props

In this chapter, you'll look at the first two techniques and how you can use them to spike your prospect's attention and create the Bed of Nails. You'll learn about the second two techniques in Chapters 11 and 12, respectively.

What-If-You Questions

Imagine for a moment that you are a prospect. Also, imagine for a moment that you are the proper target for the message in this example. (It's highly unlikely that this is the case, but the example will work better if you play along.)

What you're going to read now are the questions that a vice president of sales and marketing for a $400 million a year software company came up with after experiencing this work. He used this series of questions to create a hot opening for all of his messaging. Again, imagine that you are the right type of prospect and that you are hearing these questions for the first time.

Ready? Here goes.

What if you never had to teach another programmer another programming language?

(Pause)

And, what if you could quickly recycle code into new applications 90 percent faster?

(Pause)

And finally, what if your documentation was automatically created for you as you wrote your applications?

(Pause)

That's what you're going to see today.

Now, if you were the right type of prospect, what would you be thinking right now?

There are two reactions that are most common.

First, you might be excited. You might be imagining what your life would be like if you could do these things. You might be saying to yourself, "Wow! If I could accomplish that, it would have a huge impact."

Second, you might be skeptical. You might be saying to yourself, "There's no way that this can be done."

Either way, what do you want to see during the rest of the meeting? How and proof. The Grabber did its job as a hot opening. It created a "wow" that kept the Old Brain from going into the Hammock.

Whether your prospect is excited or skeptical, you've now changed the game. Now your prospect is leaning into your message, as opposed to begging you to stop. And those are two very different reactions.

This type of Grabber is called *what-if-you* questions. Here are some tips for delivering them well.

First, ask two or three what-if-you questions in a row. If you ask only one what-if-you question, it doesn't engage your prospect as much as you need to. If you ask four or more of these questions, it starts to feel like a technique, as opposed to a conversation.

This is an important point.

When any of the Grabber techniques are done well, they will feel very natural to your prospect, even while they're doing their job of grabbing your prospect's attention. Always keep in mind that you want these techniques to feel natural.

Another tip is to make sure that you pause after each question—long enough to give your prospect a chance to register the question and think about it for a moment. How long you pause is partly a function of culture. This work has been done in 56 different countries. Use your best judgment in choosing the pause length that feels most natural for you.

Here are two common mistakes that sales professionals make that steal the power from these questions.

The first mistake is to ask three what-if-you questions and then finish by asking, "Can you see how that would be a benefit to you?" or "Can you see how that would be an advantage for you?"

Why would closed-ended questions like these be a mistake? Because part of the power of this technique is that it gets people imagining what it's like to own your solution, and when you ask a closed-ended yes/no question, the prospect stops imagining, and that's deadly for your messaging efforts.

The second mistake sales professionals make when asking what-if-you questions is that they phrase them more like this: "What if we could do X for you? And, what if we could do Y for you? And, what if we could do Z for you?"

How are those questions different from the what-if-you questions? They substitute the word *we* for *you*. That changes the questions in a way that weakens them dramatically. This is probably obvious to you at this point, given that you read Chapter 7 on you phrasing.

Number Plays

To give you a feel for the impact that this next type of Grabber can have on your performance, there are three numbers that you should consider.

99

95

4

These three numbers have to do with golf.

$9,900,000 is the amount of winnings Tiger Woods had on the PGA Tour in 2006. And that doesn't count the money he made in endorsements.

$950,000 is the amount of winnings the *average* pro golfer had on the PGA Tour in 2006.

4 percent is the percentage of stroke/scoring difference between Tiger Woods and the average pro golfer on the PGA Tour in 2006.

Just a 4-percent difference. And what this shows is that, even if you are working in a highly competitive environment, having just a slight advantage over your competition can lead to an enormous difference in overall results.

And if you follow the coaching in this book, your ability to deliver a message will improve a lot more than 4 percent.

This is an example of another type of Grabber called a *number play*.

A number play is a more interesting way of delivering numbers as part of your message. First, you write all of the relevant numbers where the prospect can see them. You can write them on whatever is handy—a sheet of paper, a whiteboard, or a napkin. Then, you explain what each number means. This keeps the prospect engaged, because he is wondering what's coming next.

One way you can use a number play is to deliver your company information. For example, one of our customers was a company that was viewed by its prospects as being a "small" player in the market, not a substantial company. Here's the number play that this company used to change that impression quickly.

First, its representatives would write out the following numbers:

28
500
8,000
85
11/65

Then, they'd explain what the numbers mean.

28	Number of years that the company's been in business
$500 million	Amount of cash that it has in the bank
8,000	Number of happy customers

| 85 | Percent of services delivered on time and on budget (industry average is 45 percent) |
| 11/65 | $11 was the price of the initial stock offering, and today it's worth $65 after splitting twice |

Then, they'd say, "These numbers show you that our company has been a top performer for years, and that you can rely on us as a partner in the future."

With just a handful of numbers, this customer was able to transform the impression that its prospects had of the company from a "small" player in the market to a substantial partner. Imagine how many PowerPoint slides that might have taken in the past.

By the way, now that you've seen some of these techniques, you'll start to notice that they are used in a lot of different places. The next time you look at a newspaper, you might notice a number play being used (often in the bottom left-hand corner of the first page of a section). You'll start to notice number plays in magazines and on the Web. You'll see these techniques all over the place because they work to gain that most precious of commodities—your attention.

While using number plays to share your company information can be effective, the best number plays provoke your prospects to see their world in a new way. The way you accomplish that is by sharing information with your prospects that they didn't know before. The more unexpected the information you provide, the more you break the pattern of what they expected to get out of their meeting with you. Remember, breaking the pattern is the key to getting people's attention and keeping them out of the Hammock.

Here's one more number play to give you a feel for how it works.

In addition to helping companies and sales professionals come up with the message they take to prospects, companies also come to us to learn how to create tools that sales professionals will actually use.

If you were to see us message to a prospect on the subject of helping her to create better sales tools, you'd see us use this number play.

90

40

∞

90   According to a recent study, up to 90 percent of all marketing materials go unused by salespeople.

Spoken: Now, you might think that is because salespeople just don't need tools from Marketing in order to communicate their message to prospects. But another study showed . . .

40   The average salesperson spends 40 hours a month creating his own marketing materials.

Spoken: So, it's not that your salespeople don't need materials. It's just that, in most companies, they're not being provided with the right materials. Plus, think of all the wasted effort in both your sales and marketing teams when you have this kind of disconnect between these two organizations. And this leads to the last challenge, which is . . .

∞   The number of different messages that are being delivered to your prospects today.

Spoken: This is what causes message schizophrenia in the market. This is why you get the stories of a sales manager saying that she traveled with three different reps, and it sounded like each rep was working for a different company. This is why companies are coming to us. They want to stop the wasted effort and the message schizophrenia.

What's powerful about this number play is that it surprises prospects at first. They wouldn't have guessed that these are the real numbers. However, once they see the numbers written in front of them, and once they really think about their situation, you start to see them nod their heads as they accept the idea that this accurately describes a core problem they are experiencing today.

When you can create a number play like that, not only have you got something that will grab your prospect's attention, but you also have something that will survive your leaving the room. You've got a message that will be memorable and a technique that your prospects will be telling their colleagues, writing on whiteboards and cafeteria napkins, and putting in their e-mails.

There's another Grabber technique that you need to learn. It takes something that you're probably doing today (sharing customer stories with your prospects) and dramatically increases the persuasive power of those stories. It deserves its own chapter.

CHAPTER 11

Stories with Contrast: Help Them See Value

A short while back, Erik was in the ballroom of a Chicago hotel, listening to sales reps try on their company's new "pitch." He'd been invited there by the CMO to evaluate this company's new message (we weren't involved in its creation) and see if we could do anything to help ensure the success of the message as it was rolled out.

Picture a ballroom filled with big, round tables that could seat eight to ten people. At each table, sales reps took turns delivering the new message to the others at that table. It was a way for them to see how it felt and hear how it sounded.

The message was a good one. You get to hear a lot of messages when you're in our line of work, and this message was well put together.

What was obvious in the reps' delivery of the message was their lack of excitement in delivering it. It was a good, logical message. But it was clear that it was going to need some more help if it was to be successful in the field.

The challenge was that the message, while logically strong, was dry. Desert dry.

If you looked at the individual components, they were all there. The message included relevant pieces of data. It was tied into the customers' business objectives and pain points. It was a simple way of explaining a complex software platform. It even had some differentiation in it.

Nonetheless, the message was forgettable.

And if nothing was done to change it, the message would not have the impact the company wanted. They had invested millions in the development of the message (so the managers told us). They were bringing in reps from around the country to participate in these message rollout events. So, the big concern was, how can we get this to stick—first with all the sales reps, and then with prospects?

Now, if you have a trained ear, and you know what to listen for, it was pretty obvious where the messaging could be improved substantially. It was in the telling of the customer stories that were used to support the message.

One of the big problems was that the customer stories weren't really stories at all. Instead, they were just data dumps in another form.

Recognizing that they had both a problem and an opportunity, this company invested energy and effort in improving their customer stories. After working with us, they had a formula for creating customer stories that persuade. And, in the process, they took a forgettable data dump and turned it into a series of memorable stories that help their message be remembered. The company made sure that their message survived their sales reps leaving the room.

Breaking Through Prospect Denial

Customer stories are one of your great opportunities to take something that you are already doing—sharing customer testimonials—and do it in a way that gets your prospect's attention. This next Grabber technique is called *customer stories with contrast.*

Telling customer stories *well* works for getting attention, even in the most challenging selling situation you'll ever face.

What's the opposite of attention when it comes to sales messaging?

It's not inattention, although that is the most logical, obvious answer. Inattention is a passive, natural occurrence that you have to wrestle with in every messaging situation. And certainly, the failure to move somebody from inattention to attention is a primary killer of sales opportunities.

But there is something that is even more of a polar opposite of attention than simple inattention. What's worse than inattention is *active resistance* to your message. What's worse than inattention is denial—your prospect's denial that he has a problem that needs solving in the first place.

All other challenges pale in comparison to this one.

The world's best selling situation is the rare time when you are able to solve a problem that a prospect has already recognized and wants solved. That's sweet living. It's also uncommon.

The more common situation is that you are able to solve a problem that the customer feels some pain around, but it's still going to take some selling to get him to feel the pain vividly enough to want to fix it.

That brings you back to the worst situation—denial.

When a prospect is in denial, your normal approaches won't work. For example, you can question him to try to uncover his pain, but if he doesn't believe he has a problem, your questions will get you nowhere. The same thing goes for your proof. The prospect who is in denial doesn't care whether you can prove your claims. So what? He doesn't believe that he has a problem in the first place.

In a great selling environment, you might be able to ignore those prospects that are in denial. But too often, you are not in a great selling environment. You need to work every prospect from every angle. You need to create opportunities.

So, how do you deal with the difficult problem of denial? Sometimes, you need to look beyond the immediately obvious to find solutions to thorny problems.

For example, imagine the insights you could get from an organization that has spent its entire history selling to prospects who are in denial that they have the problem you solve. Like studying creatures that have evolved specialized features to deal with their unique environments, studying an organization that deals only with people who are in denial might give you insights into how to deal with the problem in your selling environment.

What Can You Learn from Alcoholics Anonymous?

One place you might look for solutions is Alcoholics Anonymous (AA), which solves a problem that almost no one is willing to admit to. And AA has done this successfully for decades. What lessons can you learn from them?

AA teaches that when someone is in denial, you can't win him over with facts. You can't convince him with data. Every time you try, the walls go up. The person says, "That's not me. I don't have that problem."

It's the same thing that happens to you when your prospect says, "I don't have a security problem on my network," or, "We don't need better processes," or, "We've got good visibility into our situation/data/environment already."

So, how does AA solve the denial problem? With stories—stories told by its members. Stories that don't engage in rational argument, such as, "You are an alcoholic; you match the profile."

What Alcoholics Anonymous has learned is that denial isn't overcome by logic. That's because denial is an identity problem. The AA prospect doesn't want to believe that he is like "those" people who are alcoholics.

This is why AA meetings start with members taking turns telling their stories.

The stories that AA uses are its members' "before" stories—what their lives were like before they came to AA, and how they came to learn they were alcoholics.

And through the telling of those stories, people who are in denial start to see themselves. And that's when they move from denial to admitting that they have a problem. They do so only when they connect with a story.

Okay, so what does this mean to you when you're selling to a prospect who is in denial. (BTW, this also works on any prospect that you're trying to persuade to move from the status quo toward your solution.)

Most people use customer stories as Proof points, not to persuade or sell. You may think that you're using them to persuade, but if you use them the way most salespeople do, then you're wrong. The stories are Proof points that your solution works, but they don't convince prospects that they have a problem that they are denying or perhaps not recognizing.

Again, look at the example of AA. AA doesn't lead with, "AA saved my life," or, "AA has helped me pull my life together." Instead, AA leads with, "I didn't think I had a problem. It started with just a couple of drinks on the weekend. Then, it became just a couple of drinks every day." And the story continues from there, describing what the storyteller's life was like before he realized that he had a problem. Through the telling of the "before" story, those who are in denial see themselves.

You need to do the same thing with your customer stories. You need to tell the story of your customers' situation *before* they implemented your solution. It's through the before story that your prospect who is in denial will start to see his own company's story.

It's not the frontal assault of logic and data that overcomes denial. It's the power of a story that never triggers the "denial" barriers in the first place.

A well-told story sucks your prospect in. He finds himself living in this other customer's story. He has an emotional response to the challenges that this other customer faced and how this other customer solved the problem that caused those challenges. One customer of ours, after years of using this technique, told his peers, "When you do this well, you've already closed the deal before you've even shown them your solution."

Value Lies in the Contrast

It's not enough just to tell the "before" story. You also need to tell the "after" story.

The contrast between the two creates a powerful perception of value. In fact, you've been told to sell on "value" for your entire sales career, but the only way the Old Brain—the decision maker—perceives value is through contrast. The bigger the contrast you can create between the "pain" the customer experienced before your solution and the "gain" the customer experienced with your solution, the greater the perceived value.

That's why this technique isn't called customer stories. It's called customer stories with contrast.

Here's an example of how a student of this work used a customer story with contrast to close an important deal.

First, some context: this salesperson was selling a piece of equipment that used a laser to measure camshafts accurately. A camshaft is a part that goes into a car engine. If it's not made perfectly, the engine will fail.

When you're selling this type of equipment in the United States, you normally focus on the Big Three—Chrysler, GM, and Ford. As this salesperson was learning about Ford's business, he got the opportunity to see how the company was testing camshafts in its plants at that time. Then, armed with how it was doing things, he got the opportunity to present to the actual decision makers at Ford.

So, picture a room with about 10 people from Ford sitting around a table. In the front of the room is the salesperson and two flip charts.

In preparing for this meeting, the salesperson's discovery with Ford had shown him that the challenges they faced were very similar to the challenges that Chrysler had been facing before Chrysler had bought this same solution earlier in the year.

So, the salesperson decided to start his presentation by telling the story of what things were like at Chrysler before Chrysler started using his solution, and also what things were like after Chrysler started using his solution.

(One quick thing about this example. This salesperson was going to share a story about Chrysler with Ford. You might be thinking, "How could he do that? They are competitors." He had permission from Chrysler to share the story. Also, this technique does not depend on using a competitor's story with a prospect. What makes this technique work is the contrast.)

After several months of unsuccessfully trying to sell the laser device to Ford's plant managers, this salesperson knew that he needed to change his approach. Every time he presented, the decision was driven to price. So this is how he changed his message by using a customer story with contrast visually displayed on two flip charts.

Keep in mind that he wrote the supporting elements out as he spoke.

[Starting on left flip chart.]

Let's take a look at what this product did for Chrysler. Before this solution, in a single facility, Chrysler had an 8 percent scrap rate. They needed to have a minimum of 24 hours of inventory on hand. And they had to replace 60 bad engines per month.

[Move to right flip chart.]

With this solution, Chrysler was able to reduce its scrap to 4 percent. They were able to reduce their inventory from 24 hours to 1 hour. Out of all these numbers, this is the one I'm most proud of: after installing our solution, Chrysler went from 60 engines replaced to 0 engines replaced.

The reduction in the scrap rate led to a savings of $360,000 the first year. The reduction in inventory led to a savings of $40,000 per month. And the engines? That was a savings of $1,200,000 the first year. Chrysler saved in excess of $1.5 million in one year with an investment of only $275,000.

This is what the flip charts looked like after he had told the story:

Chrysler Before	Chrysler Today
8% Scrap rate	4% Scrap rate ($360,000)
24 hours Inv.	1 hour Inv. ($40,000/mo)
60 bad eng/mo.	0 bad eng/mo. ($1,200,000)
	Savings $1,500,000+
	Investment $275k

At this point in the presentation, a Ford executive stood up and said to the group, "We'll take two. Do you realize that we have the same exact thing happening at two of our plants today?"

This is what happens when you create value up front. There was no focus on the cost of the product. The product cost $275,000, and the salesman hadn't even demoed the equipment.

When you use stories with contrast, the value is easy to understand because it lies in the contrast between the prospect's current pain and the gain associated with your solution.

Stories with contrast, at their most basic level, contain three elements:

1. *Pain.* What was the challenge the customer was facing? In the case of Chrysler, it was a scrap rate that was too high. In addition, the company had to carry a lot of goods in inventory. And finally, even though the company was testing the camshafts, some bad camshafts still ended up in engines. So, you can easily imagine the problems that were created in the dealer channel and from a customer satisfaction standpoint.

2. *Gain.* What did the customer get by moving to your solution? Chrysler was able to reduce its scrap rate by half, dramatically reduce the amount of goods it had to carry in inventory, and eliminate bad engines resulting from camshaft failure.

3. *Proof.* What was the impact of these changes? In Chrysler's situation, it was able to save more than $1,500,000 for an investment of only $275,000.

Now, suppose that instead of putting up Chrysler's numbers, the salesperson had instead put up Ford's numbers and never talked about Chrysler at all. Would his presentation have had the same impact? When you ask this question to a room full of people, they always say, "No. It wouldn't have had the same impact." When you ask why, they say, "Because the Chrysler story is the proof."

This is interesting. Think about how hard sales professionals work to prove their claims today. You look for third-party information. You try to do proof of concepts and pilots. You set up site visits or invest in demonstration centers. These are all very expensive proof sources that lengthen sales cycles.

What great salespeople understand is that one well-told customer story with contrast is worth 1,000 points of data.

Contrast this approach with using an ROI (return on investment) calculator. Many salespeople use ROI calculators to convince prospects to buy their solution. But how much impact do these calculators really have?

When you break out your ROI calculator and show your prospect the numbers, does he say, "Oh, why didn't you just start with this? I'll take two."

No. When you use an ROI calculator with a prospect, what usually happens? He starts to argue with the assumptions in the model.

What's different about using another customer's story is that if the prospect wants to argue with the numbers, who is he arguing with? Not with you. He's arguing with the other company (Chrysler in this example).

Another way of looking at this technique is like this. Imagine that this sales rep had used Ford's numbers instead of Chrysler's. He certainly could have done that. He'd done his homework. He knew what Ford's numbers for scrap rate, inventory, and bad engines were.

What if instead of using Chrysler's numbers, he had just put up the Ford numbers on flip charts? Imagine that when he put up the 8 percent scrap rate, there was someone in the room from Ford who was responsible for scrap rate. And this person knew that Ford's scrap rate wasn't 8 percent; it was more like 7.25 percent. What might have happened then?

Well, the person from Ford might have started arguing about the numbers, even though the difference isn't big enough to matter, right? Because whether it's 8 percent or 7.25 percent, if Ford could get its scrap rate down to 4 percent, that would be a big enough gain to make it worth the change. But, all of a sudden you are lost in the weeds in an argument that derails the point and the power of the conversation.

One thing that's great about the customer-story-with-contrast technique is that it takes away the natural defensiveness that your prospect might have. Rather than saying, "Here are the areas where you are falling down," the technique helps you change the game. It's as if you are coming over to your prospect's side of the table and saying, "Let's take a look at what's happening at this customer over here." It puts you in a more consultative position.

There are three additional things you can do to improve your customer stories.

1. Tell a story.
2. Use telling details.
3. Make the customer the hero.

One of the things that causes many customer stories to lose their impact is that they aren't actually stories. They're really just data dumps in another form.

In preparation for some messaging work with a multi-billion-dollar software firm, we received 100 customer stories to review. If you had read those customer stories, you would have noticed that they were missing one important element: human beings.

They read like one robot company had worked with another robot company and produced some robot results. There was no sense of real people being frustrated with the way things were before the company solved its problem, and there was no sense of people being happy with the new way things were being done after the company bought this solution.

It's the difference between telling a story and presenting data. In his book *A Whole New Mind*, Dan Pink explains the difference between facts and a story this way. He writes, "A fact is 'The queen died and the king died.' A story is 'The queen died and the king died of a broken heart.'"

When you tell customer stories, don't be afraid to link data with emotion. Often the best way to do that is to talk about the people who were affected by the challenging environment that they were working in. Then, talk about how their lives became better, easier, more fun, or less stressful after using your solution.

Another way to make your customer stories better is to use "telling details." Using telling details cures one of the big challenges in customer stories—the failure to be interesting.

If you look at the way most customer stories are put together, it's like Mad Libs. You might remember Mad Libs from when you were a kid. Mad Libs were those books that had stories in them with lots of blanks. Your job was to get someone who couldn't see what the sentence was to fill in the blanks. So, you might say, "I need a noun. Okay, now I need a verb. Now I need an adjective." Then you'd put your friends' answers into the blanks, and it would a make a (sometimes) funny story.

Often customer stories are put together the same way—with no attempt to be interesting, let alone funny. The format that's used is something like this:

> (Fill-in blank) customer is a (fill-in blank) company. It has been in business (fill-in blank) years. It has (fill-in blank) locations. It makes, sells, and services (fill-in blank) solutions.

And on, and on, and on.

This creates stories with too much information that say nothing (or very little) that's important.

The more powerful way to tell a customer story is through the use of telling details. *Telling details* are pieces of information that tell you a lot with just a few words.

Tom Wolfe, the author of *The Bonfire of the Vanities* and *The Right Stuff*, put it this way in an interview. He said, "You can tell a lot about a character just by the shoes he's wearing."

What would be an example of a telling detail in a customer story? Here are a few.

We were working with a company that supplies filter bags to businesses like cement companies. These filter bags are similar to the ones you have in a vacuum cleaner, but obviously are much larger and more highly engineered. They go inside of the "baghouse" for these big pieces of equipment.

When we worked with the company on its customer stories, they gave us one that was pretty good. It had contrast and proof, but it was a little dry.

After the salesperson had finished sharing the story, and we were moving on to another story, he turned to the person next to him and said, "You know what I love about this customer? Before they started using our bags, they used to have what they called 'baghouse parties' once a month. (This was a big joke, like a moving party or something else that nobody wants to do.) They would make a bunch of their people come in on the weekends and change out the old filter bags."

Interestingly, as far as this salesperson was concerned, he'd already given us what we needed to know about this customer story. But we jumped on this concept of "baghouse parties" immediately. We asked if the customer had to hold those baghouse parties anymore now that they had started using this salesperson's solution, and the salesperson said no.

Baghouse parties is an example of a telling detail. When you can tell a customer story by saying that the company used to have to hold baghouse parties once a month, and now they don't have to hold them anymore, you've told your customer a tremendous amount in very few words. Your customer can imagine what that situation must have been like, and what it would mean to have that problem go away.

When we worked with a company that has a software platform for managing time, labor, and benefits, one of the stories they wanted to work on was about their impact on a large health-care organization. They told that story like so many others: the customer had (fill-in blank) locations, specialized in (fill-in blank) medicine, and so on.

But while we were working on the story with people from the company, they told us (almost in passing) that this health-care organization had won an award as one of the top places in the United States for nurses to work. Remember, what our customer did was implement time, labor, and benefits solutions. Here's what we coached their salespeople to say:

> To give you a feel for the impact this technology can have on your hospital, imagine that you have just received the Magnet Award for excellence in nursing. . . What else could you do to create an even better nursing environment than you'd already put in place? That's what this customer came to us to do. They had already won the Magnet Award. But, their managers knew that there was still an opportunity to improve the work environment for the organization's nurses, and they chose our solution.

The customer story automatically becomes more interesting because it's about an organization that has won the Magnet Award, but still thinks they can improve by using this service.

The third thing you can do to make your customer stories with contrast even stronger is to make the customer the hero of the story.

You learned about the hero model of storytelling in Chapter 8. It applies here, as well.

Imagine that you're a prospect, and a salesperson starts telling you a story about one of her customers. As the salesperson tells the story, you hear that the customer had been all messed up before the salesperson got there. The customer had made a bunch of bad decisions, and it was hurting their business. Then, the salesperson showed up, found the problem, and rescued this poor customer.

What might you be thinking at this moment? You might be wondering to yourself, if I were to do business with this salesperson, how would she describe my situation to other people? Would she describe me as hopeless? As someone she had to rescue?

Would you want to do business with that salesperson? Would it feel safe? Or would it feel as if you might risk your reputation because of the story the salesperson would tell others?

When you tell customer stories with contrast, remember to keep the customer the hero of the story. You'll still get credit for being part of the solution, and you won't risk alienating the prospect that you're talking to.

Last point: when you work on your customer stories with contrast, there is an easy test to see if you're telling your customer story as a *story*.

Tell it to a peer, and then ask him to tell it back to you. If you told it as a story, he will be able to repeat every important element with ease. If he can't, then you didn't tell a story. You dumped data.

When it comes to breaking patterns, what-if-you questions, number plays, and stories with contrast are great, but the Grabber technique in the next chapter might be more powerful than any of them.

CHAPTER 12

3D Props: Are You Serious?

You may not be old enough to remember this, but when the *Challenger* space shuttle disaster happened, there was a lot of mystery around what had caused it. As a result, President Reagan put together a presidential commission to investigate the cause of the accident.

On the commission were a wide variety of people. Some of them were from NASA, and the people from NASA had an agenda. It was to make sure that they didn't get blamed for the accident.

There were also some independent outsiders on the committee. One of them was a man named Richard Feynman.

Richard Feynman was one of the most brilliant physicists who ever lived. He won the Nobel Prize in physics. One of his peers described Feynman's approach to problem solving as having three steps:

- Identify the problem.
- Think hard.
- Solve the problem.

Feynman was a genuine genius.

Feynman had a theory about what had caused the *Challenger* disaster. He believed that it was too cold on the morning of the launch. As a result, the rubber O-rings that sealed the booster rockets failed, causing a leak, and it was this leak that caused the explosion.

The problem was that the people from NASA didn't want that to be the answer because engineers from Morton Thiokol had warned them about that risk before the shuttle was launched. So, every time Feynman tried to bring up his theory during committee meetings, the people from NASA would dismiss it and take the conversation in another direction. Feynman knew that his argument wasn't gaining traction, and that if he didn't do something to force the committee's hand, his theory wouldn't be investigated. So, here's what he did.

The committee hearings were being televised live during the day. The soap operas and other daytime shows were interrupted as the nation followed the investigation.

As he headed to one of the hearings, Feynman brought a C-clamp with him—one of those C-shaped metal clamps that you use to put pressure on something or hold something in place. He also had a piece of rubber O-ring.

When he got to the hearing, he took the clamp and tightened it on the piece of rubber O-ring until the O-ring had an hourglass shape. Then he asked for a cup of ice water.

He dropped the O-ring and the clamp into the cup of ice water and waited for it to be his turn to speak. When it was his turn, he reached into the cup of ice water, pulled out the clamp and the O-ring, and said:

> So, I took this stuff [holding up the O-ring and clamp], and I put it in ice water. And I discovered that when you put some pressure on it for a while and then undo it [he releases the

pressure on the O-ring and hands it to another committee member], it doesn't stretch back; it stays the same dimension. In other words, for a few seconds at least, and more seconds than that, there's no resilience in this particular material when it's at a temperature of 32 degrees. I believe that has some significance for our problem.

He then gave more details about his theory that it was the O-ring failure that had caused the disaster.

Now, this was literally 30 seconds of testimony (you can see it on YouTube) out of several hours of testimony that day. But, what were the 30 seconds of testimony that every major news broadcast started with that evening? Feynman's home-made demonstration. As a result, the American people rallied to Feynman's cause, and his theory is now the accepted explanation for why the *Challenger* disaster happened.

But what if, instead of doing that demonstration, Feynman had presented his theory using spreadsheets and talking about how O-rings perform under different pressure and temperatures? Would it have had the same impact? Almost certainly not.

Feynman took advantage of one of the most powerful techniques you have to deliver your message in a memorable way. He used a prop to tell his story.

Prop Up Your Message

A few years ago, a student of this work used a funnel as a prop.

He was selling a solution that helped companies get sales leads through the Web and then routed those leads to the appropriate salesperson in the company. This meant that his target prospect was marketing departments—in particular, the vice president of marketing.

Vice presidents of marketing spend a lot of time thinking about the sales funnel. The *sales funnel* is a way of describing the fact that there's a universe of suspects out there who have the potential to become prospects. Once you make contact with them and qualify them, they become prospects and go into the top of your sales funnel.

During the selling process, some of them will drop out for a variety of reasons—no budget, bad timing, loss to competition, and so on. And some will stay in the funnel and move all the way through the sales process to close. So, the wide top of the funnel represents all of your qualified prospects, and the narrower bottom of the funnel represents all of your closed deals.

In many organizations, the VP of marketing is responsible for getting as many qualified leads into the top of that funnel as possible. So, when this salesperson had a meeting with a VP of marketing and her staff, after introductions, he would start out the meeting this way:

> [Holding up a funnel and setting it down in front of the VP of marketing] When you think of a funnel in the context of your job today, what do you normally think of?

The VP would almost always say something like, "I think of the sales funnel. My job is to get as many leads into the top of that funnel as possible." And the salesperson would respond:

I'm not surprised to hear you say that. In fact, most VPs of marketing tell us that exact same thing. Now, what if you could triple the number of leads that went into the top of that funnel? And what if each of those leads was instantly routed to the appropriate sales rep, so it didn't get stale because it was sitting on somebody's desk or in a drawer somewhere? And what if you could do all of that without adding any new headcount to your staff? That's what I wanted to talk to you about today.

And then he would continue with the meeting. The meeting would come to an end, and he'd leave. And then, a week or two later, he would do a follow-up meeting at the office of the VP of marketing. And what do you think he'd see, either on her desk or on a shelf somewhere in her office? The funnel.

What's that funnel doing for him the whole time he's not in the room? It's selling for him—reminding the VP why she needs his solution.

And that's the great thing about props. Props are memorable.

There is also a potentially bad thing about props. Props are memorable.

The thing to remember is that you need to use props to make an important point. If you don't, you run the risk that they'll seem silly or cute, and that's not what you want.

By the way, you use props all the time when you're talking to people you like. If you've ever been at a lunch and explained something to someone by moving glasses of water around to show how it works, you've used props. You just need to use them consciously when you're communicating your message to clients.

Props are a great way of breaking the pattern of what your prospect expects. They are a great way of creating that Bed of Nails that you learned about in the Hammock chapter.

If you were to see our own salespeople messaging to a prospect, you might see them use a piece of paper as a prop. The situation would be something like this. After some initial conversation about who we are, when it's time to explain why companies come to us, you'd see our rep rip a piece of paper out of a notebook and say:

> Imagine that this piece of paper represents all the information that your salespeople need to communicate to their prospects about your company. The question is, how much of that information will your prospects remember after your salespeople leave the room? The science says that one hour after your salespeople leave the room, the average person can remember about 50 percent of what the sales reps had to say. [Our rep folds the paper in half to represent 50 percent of the message remembered.] Just eight hours after your reps leave the room, your prospects can remember about 25 percent of what they had to say. [The rep folds the paper in half again.] Just 72 hours after they leave the room, the science shows that your prospects can remember about 10 percent of what your reps had to say. [The rep folds the paper in half again, plus a little bit more to represent 10 percent.] And just one week later? [The rep tries hard to fold the paper, but can't fold it anymore.] There's not enough strength in my fingertips to reduce this paper down to how much the average person can remember from one of your salespeople's conversations.

So, the question is . . . does it have to be like that? And the answer is, no, it doesn't. The human brain is not wired to remember facts and data. But it is wired to remember stories—information wrapped in emotion. And when you can take all of the complex information that your reps need to communicate and turn it into a simple, differentiated, and memorable story, you dramatically change how much of your message is remembered. [The rep opens that paper back up while talking.] And of course, what's the point of having the meeting if your message doesn't get remembered? That's why companies are coming to us.

Tomorrow's *Wall Street Journal*

Props can take many forms. Sometimes the best prop is a metaphor or analogy that is made tangible. Another student of our work used the *Wall Street Journal* as a prop.

She was attempting to sell a payroll and benefits system to a midsize company. At the meeting were the prospect company's president and several of his VPs.

She started the meeting by holding up a *Wall Street Journal* and asking, "How much is today's *Wall Street Journal* worth?" She wasn't trying to make it tough for them, so she held the paper so that it was easy for them to see that it was worth $2. Someone gave the right answer. To which she said, "Right, today's *Wall Street Journal* is worth $2. Now, how much would a *Wall Street Journal* from last week be worth today?" Someone said that it wouldn't be worth anything. She agreed saying, "Right. Yesterday's news isn't very valuable."

And then she asked, "But how much would tomorrow's *Wall Street Journal* be worth, if you could have it today?" The people in the room broke out in grins, and they said that it would be worth a lot of money. And she said, "Yeah, getting tomorrow's information today is highly valuable. And what you're about to see is how with this system you'll be able to get tomorrow's information today." She then continued with the meeting.

At the end of the meeting, she wrapped up by asking, "So, what do you think?" And the president of this company got up from where he was sitting, walked around the table to pick up the *Wall Street Journal*, turned to his VPs, and said, "All I know is we can't keep running this business based on yesterday's news." As you can imagine, this salesperson was feeling pretty confident at this point in the sales cycle.

One of the interesting challenges in this work is what happens when you bring it to countries outside of the United States, which we've been doing for more than 20 years (56 countries to date). Sometimes the first reaction from international audiences is that this is "American stuff." But the reality is that these techniques work anytime, anywhere, with any audience.

A few years back, one of our consultants was delivering this work in India. During a break, one of the participants came up to him and said, "You're doing a great job. But there's one thing you should know. Props will never work in India. It just won't work culturally."

Our consultant responded by thanking the participant for letting him know and admitting that he didn't know that much about India. The consultant said that, in fact, most of what he knew about India was centered on Gandhi. Then our consultant added, "You know, when I think about it, almost every picture I ever saw of Gandhi had him standing next to something, and I'm having trouble remembering what that thing was."

The Indian gentleman jumped in, saying, "It was a spinning wheel." And our consultant said, "Yeah, that's right. It was a spinning wheel." And then he said, "And it was supposed to represent something, right? What was it supposed to represent?" Again the Indian gentleman responded, "It was supposed to represent our people's ability to take care of ourselves. And, that we didn't need to have the British ruling over the top of us."

And our consultant said, "Yeah, now I remember." And then the consultant finished his point, "The only other thing I know about India is its flag. Your flag has just one symbol on it, right?" At this point the Indian gentleman is starting to get it, and he says, "Yes." And our consultant asks, "And what is that symbol?" And the Indian gentleman replies, "A spinning wheel." Of course, this made the point that not only can props work in India, but indeed the entire country was based around a noble idea represented by a prop.

You've learned several techniques that you can use to create a Bed of Nails that will keep your prospects and customers out of the Hammock. You can now take the message you created with your Power Positions and make it more memorable. But there's another technique you need to learn that will do more than any other to simplify your message, while at the same time making it stick. If you think of Grabbers as the wow of your message, this next technique shows your prospect the how in the most compelling and simple way possible. That's what the next chapter is all about.

CHAPTER 13

Big Pictures: Make the Abstract Concrete and the Complex Simple

When is a sales pitch worth more than $10 billion?

The bid to be the site for the 2016 Summer Olympics was down to the final four cities: Chicago, Madrid, Tokyo, and Rio de Janeiro. An Olympic Games Committee survey conducted by Credit Suisse set the financial value of winning the games at more than $10 billion.

Three of the cities had reason to be optimistic. Chicago had President Obama backing it, and a lot of press attention was being given to the amount of personal energy that President Obama was investing to try to bring the Olympics to his hometown. Tokyo and Madrid were the top two scorers during the Applicant Phase of the original seven cities to even attempt a bid for the games.

And then there was Rio.

Rio had failed in its bid to be an Olympic site for 2004 and 2012. It hadn't even been a finalist either time. And whenever talk of its potential as a host city for the Olympics was discussed, the conversation inevitably centered on Rio's relatively high crime rate.

To win the bid, Rio needed to come up with a reason why it was uniquely suited to be the next host city. And it needed to make sure that its message was delivered with impact.

The presentations took place in Copenhagen, with each city getting an opportunity to make its case.

The presenter from Rio stood before the International Olympic Committee (IOC) with a blank map of the world behind him. After some introductory remarks, he said:

> Today, the Olympic movement is looking for new ways to reach the youth of the world and to spread our global message. . . . Personally, I have seen wonderful Olympic and Paralympic Games in Europe [behind the speaker, the map filled up with the names of the cities on those continents that had hosted the games—there were so many that you almost couldn't see Europe anymore], in Asia, in Oceania, and in North America [the map filled up the names of the cities in those continents that had hosted the games]. . . . In modern Olympic history, there have been 30 games in Europe [a big number 30 goes on the map over the top of Europe], 5 in Asia, 2 in Oceania, and 12 in North America [a big number goes up over each of those continents].

At this point, one thing was glaringly obvious: neither Africa nor South America had hosted any Olympic Games in the modern Olympic era. Those two continents were untouched by the Olympic movement. And only one of the four cities bidding for the 2016 Summer Olympic Games could fix that problem.

We want to bring the games to South America for the first time, and open the door to a new continent. [Rio showed up on the map with an Olympic logo.] One that stands ready to take the Olympic movement forward to new territories and new cultures and people and, thanks to the character and the spirit of Rio—a new energy.

Against great odds, Rio won the bid to host the 2016 Summer Olympic Games. When the members of the IOC were asked why they had voted for Rio, they all mentioned the fact that Rio represented an opportunity to bring the Olympics to a continent that had never seen them. They all mentioned the map. And what the delegation from Rio did with that map is an example of the next technique you will learn.

Using Big Pictures

You've learned how to find your Power Positions, which are the bones of your story. You've also learned how to use Grabbers to create some "wow" to get your prospect's attention. What you're going to learn next is a technique that shows your prospects *how* you're going to get this done for them.

There is no more powerful technique than this one for simplifying a complex message. It's called Big Pictures.

When people speaking standard American English say that they're going to give you *the big picture*, what they usually mean is that they are going to talk at you for a while. But that's not what you're hearing from us when you hear the words *Big Picture*.

Big Picture means a visual that you can draw, not just words. You've seen numerous examples of Big Pictures from us throughout this book: the sideways "T" picture about changing the status quo, the Value Wedge Big Picture, the Message Pyramid, and the Hammock are all examples of the Big Picture technique.

All of the visuals in this book take complex concepts and simplify them through the use of the visual. The Big Pictures help to explain a concept in the moment, as well as making the concept easier to remember later.

Now, if you were to travel around with us delivering this work, you would sometimes hear people challenge the idea that they need to use Big Pictures to help them tell their story. These doubters often say that there are two reasons why they don't need to use Big Pictures.

One reason they believe that they don't need to use Big Pictures is that the way they speak is very clear. So, why would they need to use a visual to support what they're saying? The other reason they believe they don't need to use Big Pictures is that their prospects are smart people. The implication is that only unintelligent people need a visual to help them understand a concept.

So, here is what you need to know. The reason you should use Big Pictures has nothing to do with how good you are at talking, and it has nothing to do with how smart your prospects are. The reason you need to use Big Pictures is that they *simplify a complex message* and *make abstract ideas concrete.*

If you were asked to think of an apple, you could do it easily. Why? Because you've experienced apples with your senses.

You've probably done some combination of touching, tasting, seeing, and smelling an apple. You've even heard the crunching sound that an apple makes when you bite into it. And because you've experienced an apple with your senses, the *idea* of an apple is concrete for you. That's what *concrete* means. It means that you've experienced something (in this case, an apple) with at least one of your five senses.

An *abstract idea* is different from a concrete idea in that it is something that you've never experienced with your senses. An example of an abstract idea would be increased efficiency or improved productivity. Those are things that you can't experience with your senses. The challenge for most sales professionals is that what they are selling today are abstract ideas, and the problem with selling abstract ideas is that people are not as motivated by abstract ideas as they are by things that are concrete.

As an example of the power of a concrete idea versus an abstract idea, a few years back the former chief of staff at Cedars-Sinai hospital in Los Angeles was on a cruise in the South Seas. It was one of those cruises where you stop at different ports throughout the trip, get off for a day of sightseeing, and then get back on the boat.

He noticed something surprising during the trip. Once you got off the boat to visit the port, the crew made you wash your hands with antibacterial soap before you could get back on the boat. And then, when you were on the boat, while you waited in line for the buffets, again the crew would pass around the antibacterial soap. By the time his vacation was over, this former chief of staff at Cedars-Sinai began to ask himself, "Is it possible that this cruise ship is actually more sanitary than my own hospital?"

So, he went back to Cedars-Sinai and decided to investigate how well the hospital was doing on hand washing. What he found was that doctors were washing their hands only 65 percent of the time they were supposed to. That means that 35 *percent of the time, the doctors weren't washing their hands when they were supposed to.*

Have you ever heard that you can go to a hospital and end up with something worse than you went in with? This is one of the prime reasons why it happens.

Now, why do you suppose these doctors weren't washing their hands when they were supposed to? Do you think that during the seven to ten years that they were learning how to be doctors, they hadn't been told of the importance of hand washing? Obviously they had. Even kindergarteners know that it's important to wash your hands when they have germs on them.

These doctors clearly knew, at the intellectual level, that they should be washing their hands. So, why didn't they do it?

One explanation is that "bacteria on your hands" is an abstract idea. You can't feel it, taste it, smell it, see it, or hear it. And so it becomes easy to rationalize away the risk and tell yourself that you don't have bacteria on your hands. As one physician at the hospital said, "You say: 'Hey, I couldn't be carrying the bad bugs. It's the other hospital personnel.'"

Another explanation is that washing your hands can be a pain—both literally and figuratively. Hand-washing stations can be out of easy reach in some situations. And some doctors say that when you have to wash your hands a lot, it hurts.

So, you've got this problem that you can't see, and fixing the problem is going to cause you some pain and inconvenience. So, what do you do? You either ignore the problem or try to rationalize why it isn't really a problem for *you.*

Does this sound like any of your prospects? Do they have problems that aren't always easy to see, and would fixing those problems cause them some inconvenience and pain? It's one of the core challenges facing most sales efforts today.

So, how did the hospital leadership respond? The first thing it tried was an education and incentive program. E-mails were sent and posters were put up around the hospital explaining why doctors needed to wash their hands when they were supposed to. And a group of hospital staff was assigned the job of rewarding doctors who were seen doing the right thing by giving them $10 gift cards to Starbucks.

After six weeks of effort, the hospital did see an improvement. Before the training and gift card program, doctors had been washing their hands 65 percent of the time they were supposed to, and after the new program, they improved to 80 percent.

That still meant that 1 out of 5 times, doctors *were not* washing their hands when they were supposed to. This was still unacceptable.

At this point, the hospital leadership got even more creative. As the leaders shared the discouraging results of their efforts to improve hand washing at the Chief of Staff Advisory Committee, they served lunch. Then, at the end of the lunch, they gave each person a petri dish. The dishes had agar in them, a material that can be used to show whether bacteria are on the skin of someone who touches it.

The participants pressed their hands on the petri dishes, and then the dishes were cultured in a lab. The hospital leadership then took a photograph of the cultured petri dishes.

The photograph showed the doctors' bacteria-covered hands. It was pretty gruesome. You could see a perfect hand shape formed from the bacteria that was cultured in the petri dishes—the hands they'd just finished eating— lunch with. Then, this same image was used as a screen saver on every computer in the hospital.

Hand-washing compliance instantly went up to 100 percent.

So, what had the leaders at the hospital done? They'd taken the abstract idea of bacteria on your hands and made it concrete. They made it something that the doctors could see. And once the doctors could see that the problem was real, they could no longer rationalize is away. They had to fix it.

And you have the same challenge. How can you make your prospects see their own bacteria-covered hands? This is where Big Pictures can help you.

If you'll glance back at the Big Pictures you've seen in this book, you will see that most of them are about showing you your bacteria-covered hand.

The Hammock shows you your bacteria-covered hand. You see how little of your message people actually remember if you don't do something different. The Value Wedge shows you your bacteria-covered hand by showing where most salespeople message (where there is no uniqueness) and how you need to change that. The same is true of the Big Picture on changing the status quo in the second chapter of this book. It shows you that your biggest competitor may be indecision, not a specific competitor, and that competing with that takes different messages and tools.

Once you've seen those Big Pictures, they're hard to forget. And yet, what if you hadn't seen a Big Picture as each of those concepts was talked about? Would you still remember the message as clearly?

For example, if you look at the Hammock, it's really just a graph of three data points—how much people remember from the beginning, middle, and end of a message. You could have simply read the concept in a series of sentences explaining the data points, with no visual at all. But if that's how you learned the concept of the Hammock (and if you hadn't heard it described with the Hammock metaphor), would it be as memorable for you a week, a month, or a year later?

No way. And the reason for this is something called the *pictorial superiority effect.*

In his book *Brain Rules*, John Medina cites several studies that tested how pictures affect memory. One study showed that people could remember more than 2,500 pictures with more than 90 percent accuracy several days after having seen them. And their original exposure to each picture was only 10 seconds. That's incredible. Written and spoken words fail miserably in comparison. In another study cited by Medina, people could remember only about 10 percent of information delivered through the spoken word just 72 hours after hearing it. If a picture was added, however, they could remember 65 percent of the information. The simple act of using a picture to help tell your story will dramatically increase your prospect's memory of what it was you had to say.

There are many varieties of Big Pictures that you can create to support your message. Some techniques for visualizing information can require many semesters of college courses and take years to master. The good news is that creating Big Pictures doesn't have to be that difficult. What you're going to learn now are some simple rules to follow that will make sure that you always create Big Pictures that have a positive impact on your message.

One word of caution: when you see the words *Big Picture* in this book, don't think of a photograph. Photographs have their place in sales messaging, but that's not what we're talking about here. The Big Picture technique is not about using photographs. It's about creating a visual that you can draw on a napkin, a sheet of paper, a whiteboard, or a flip chart as you're talking to your customer (it could go in a slide as well, but you'll get a more in-depth discussion of using slides later in this book).

Step 1. *Make it about your customer's pains/obstacles/ challenges.* The first thing that separates a good Big Picture from a bad Big Picture is its starting point. A weak Big Picture is one that's all about your company. You may have seen these before. An example would be a visual that shows the three or four pillars (sometimes columns) of stuff your company does for customers.

"We bring you service [column 1], people [column 2], and technology [column 3]." The problem with that type of Big Picture is that it's all about *you*. What you need is a Big Picture that's all about *your customer*.

The best Big Pictures have the opposite starting point. They start by visualizing the customer's world, pains, or challenges. This is a spot where the groundwork you did when you were creating your Power Positions carries over. If you remember, you created your Power Positions by first looking at your prospects' business objectives and pains. You'll use those as a source for getting started on your Big Picture.

Again, going back to the Hammock, the first thing that this Big Picture did was talk about your pain (the fact that your messages are being forgotten by your prospects). And then we visualized that pain for you by using a simple graph. Of course, a Big Picture doesn't have to be a graph; it's just what we used in this example.

Step 2. *Contrast with the gains your customer can get from your solution.* Weak Big Pictures don't show contrast. Strong Big Pictures contrast the prospect's world today with what it will become if the prospect uses your solution. (Remember the discussion in the previous chapter on the impact of contrast and your prospect perceiving value.)

Going back to the Hammock example, the spikes are the visualization of what you will be able to do differently after using our solutions—the techniques presented in this book.

Step 3. *If you can make it work, use a metaphor to make it more memorable.* The best Big Pictures often, but not always, use a metaphor or analogy. The Hammock is made more memorable through the analogy of calling it the Hammock, since that is how it's shaped and since you're trying to make sure that people don't fall asleep during your message.

These three steps are in order of importance. If all you can do is visualize the prospect's pain, that can be enough. And it should be your top priority.

If you can then visualize the prospect's gain from working with you, you'll make your Big Picture stronger.

If you can then layer onto that a metaphor or analogy that makes it more memorable, you'll have the strongest Big Picture possible.

Picture Pitfall to Avoid

Big Pictures are a powerful technique, but it's possible to use them poorly. One of the places where people make a mistake is not taking the steps in order. What they'll do is fall in love with a metaphor and then end up trying to draw the metaphor.

For example, they might decide that their solution is like insurance (even though they're not actually selling insurance), so they try to draw an insurance certificate. Well, if you're not actually selling insurance, you aren't making your prospect any smarter by drawing a square box with the words "insurance certificate" in it. And if your prospect doesn't learn anything meaningful from your visual, it's not helping you.

Or they might decide that what they are selling provides you with peace of mind and a feeling of security. Then they think, yeah, like a pacifier for a baby! Then, they'll try to draw a pacifier. Here's the thing: if you're not selling pacifiers, this is likely to get you thrown out of your prospect's office. It's too cute, and it doesn't make your prospect smarter. A Big Picture should be the opposite of that.

Don't go for the metaphor first. Instead, first draw what your prospect's world looks like today. Then draw how your prospect's world will be different tomorrow with your solution. After you've successfully accomplished that, step back and look at the picture and ask yourself, "What does that look like?" Then, if you can, come up with a metaphor that will make it more memorable, but not before.

Here's an example of how one of our customers, Seagate, created a Big Picture to use in its messaging. It has all the elements: pain, contrasted with gain, and a metaphor to make it more memorable.

If you're not familiar with Seagate, you just need to know that for more than 30 years it has created the hard drives used in business and consumer products.

As Seagate looked at their customer's business objectives and pains, they realized that all of their prospects struggled with creating differentiated products. Those same prospects use Seagate's drive technology to create new products or to upgrade existing products. So, Seagate used a Big Picture to show customers the challenge that they faced and how Seagate could help them overcome that challenge.

First, following the distinct-point-of-view model, Seagate used some numbers to get its prospects to realize just how big the problem was. (We're leaving that out here to focus solely on the Big Picture. You just need to know that Seagate followed the distinct POV model to provoke their customers.) Having accomplished that, the company used the following Big Picture to take this abstract idea of innovation and differentiation and make it concrete.

Here are the words a salesperson might use to narrate this Big Picture.

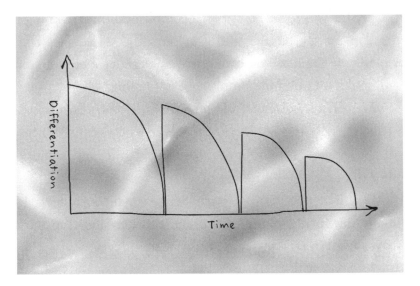

Let's look at the dynamics of this problem.

When you look at a graph of *differentiation over time,* you can see that when an innovation comes out, you can seize the opportunity and put it into your product, and that gives you some differentiation. That's great, but it doesn't last forever. There's a finite window in which you get to have that differentiation, but then your competitors catch up, and your differentiation goes down to zero.

So, what you have to do is look for the next innovation. You seize the next innovation and get additional differentiation, but, again, it lasts for only so long.

And what you're seeing is that innovation is driving less and less differentiation over time. On average, the scale of the next innovation is not as big as it used to be, and the windows in which you get to enjoy that differentiation are getting shorter and shorter as competitors get faster and faster at imitation. So, this is your challenge.

You can think of this chart as a *shark chart*. If you've seen the movie *Jaws*, you'll know this shape; it's a shark fin, and it's coming toward you—and it's picking up speed. What you need to do . . . is stay ahead of it.

This is what's happening to businesses right now, when you can't differentiate much or can only differentiate for a short period of time, you're going to experience pressure on your profit margins.

The challenge is to figure out how to stay ahead of the shark.

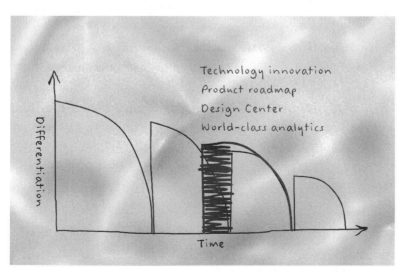

And that's why companies are coming to Seagate. Because when it comes to innovation, we can help you see what new technologies are coming and give you access to these technologies sooner.

It's like being able to push this line back. [Draws thick, darkened line.]

And when you can see an innovation coming before anyone else does, you have time to prepare, and you can get it into your product earlier and go to market quicker than anyone else. Of course, the competition will eventually react and catch up, so this will still end at some point. But you get to enjoy these higher margins for a longer period of time. You want to differentiate as early as possible, rather than being in catch-up mode. And when you do take advantage of new technologies sooner than your competition, rather than the shark threatening you, you become the shark that's taking a bite out of the competition's business.

So, how can Seagate help you do that?

Number one, we're the leader when it comes to *technology innovation* in the drive space. We're creating new technology before anybody else does. And what that means is that you can take advantage of *our road map* and learn what products we have in development, so that you know what's coming down the pike that could make a huge difference in your products.

Of course, it takes resources to take advantage of these new technologies. And not all companies have the internal staff to take advantage of the opportunity, even if they have the knowledge. This is why we provide you with *Design Center* services, so that you don't have to have all the product expertise in-house. You can use our product experts to help you.

How do you know which new technology wave is right for you? Which new innovation should you take advantage of? Because of our depth and breadth in the market, we have

160

business analytics that reach the whole storage market and can give you guidance on where to place your next bet, so that you can make that shark work for you.

After this, again following the distinct-point-of-view model, the salesperson uses a customer story as proof that Seagate can do what it claims to be able to do.

This simple visual helps Seagate deliver its message in a memorable way. It also gives the company's sales professionals the chance to show their business depth. When you can do something like this on a napkin or a whiteboard, you show that you're doing more than just being a slide jockey.

Here's another example of an effective Big Picture. This was created by a company called Omnicell. Omnicell helps health-care facilities acquire, manage, dispense, and deliver medications and supplies more effectively.

In this one, you'll see how Omnicell used the first two of the three elements for creating a Big Picture: show the pain and then contrast it with the gain. Remember that the elements of a Big Picture are in priority order. If all you do is visualize the pain, you'll have something that's very effective. If you can contrast it with a gain, it will be even more effective. The last element you might add is a metaphor that makes it more memorable. But don't force a metaphor. If you don't have one that fits, that's okay.

Like Seagate, Omnicell followed the distinct-point-of-view model. They used some numbers to get their prospects to realize just how big the problem they were facing was. Then, Omnicell used the following Big Picture to take this abstract idea and make it concrete.

Here are the words a salesperson might use to narrate this Big Picture.

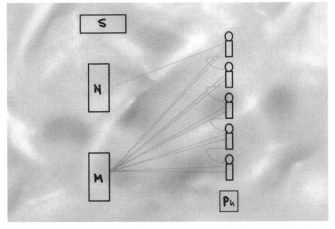

Courtesy of Omnicell.

Think about a typical medical-surgical nursing unit. Pretend for the time being that you're in California and that your nurses only have five patients to care for.

Here are the patients.

Here's your nursing station. [Draws box with N.]

Here's the med cabinet. [Draws box with M.]

There's the inconveniently located supply cabinet. [Draws box with S.]

Oh . . . and way over here?

That's the pharmacy. [Draws box with Ph.]

Okay, so maybe it's an "almost perfect" world!

In this almost-perfect-world scenario, the nurse arrives at the nursing station for a 12-hour shift and begins her rounds. She visits the first patient, assesses his needs, goes to the medication cabinet, retrieves the necessary meds, returns to administer them, and moves on to the next patient . . . and so on, until all medications have been administered and the patients are all secure and happy.

Is this how things typically run in your nursing units?

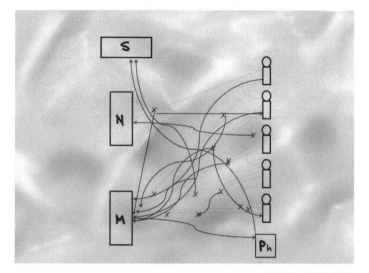

Courtesy of Omnicell.

Here's what's far more likely to happen.

Your nurse is going to be interrupted.

A lot.

In fact, according to some studies, nurses are interrupted up to 12 times an hour during a typical 12-hour daytime shift. And these interruptions can happen anywhere, for any reason. But the majority of these interruptions need to be dealt with right away.

So instead of this nice, neat, orderly almost-perfect-world scenario, your typical workflow tends to end up looking more like this.

[Draw arrows and lines as you are talking to illustrate each interruption.]

She might have to go to the medication cabinet to witness another nurse waste a narcotic. She might arrive at the medication cabinet, only to discover that the drugs she needs are missing and need to be tracked down at the pharmacy or elsewhere in the unit. Maybe she gets halfway back to the patient's room, discovers that she's grabbed the wrong med, and has to go back and get the right one. A patient in another room might desperately need his pain medication, so the nurse will have to drop everything to get the narcotics, do the count back, and administer the drug. Or, once she gets to the patient's room, she finds out that he's brought some medications from home that need to be administered, and no one seems to know where they are.

You get the idea. The point is that each of these interruptions takes time and attention away from patients.

And this has a direct impact on all three of those key components of patient satisfaction that we talked about earlier. Here's how.

First, let's look at *patient safety*.

Researchers in Australia found that each time a nurse was interrupted, it increased the chance of a clinical error by 12.7 percent. The more distractions there were, the more mistakes the nurses made.

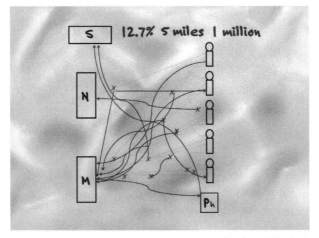

Courtesy of Omnicell.

What about the impact on *nursing efficiency*?

If you take a look at each of these squiggly lines, you'll see that every interruption forces a nurse to take a detour or go out of her way to deal with the interruption.

That kind of inefficiency also adds up to as much as 5 miles per day that a nurse has to walk *just to do her job.* And, despite all that walking, that's time that's not being spent with the patients.

Finally, consider the impact that all this has on *nursing satisfaction.* You have distracted, exhausted nurses with no control over their time who are constantly worried about making a mistake that could harm the patients they are supposed to be caring for.

Is it any wonder that the American Hospital Association is predicting a shortage of one million nurses by 2020?

Given that the quality and frequency of nursing interaction play such a key role in favorable outcomes, how can you and your nurses overcome these challenges?

What if you could minimize the number of interruptions and distractions and their impact on your nurses' workflow? How would this help you enhance patient safety, increase nursing efficiency, and improve nursing satisfaction?

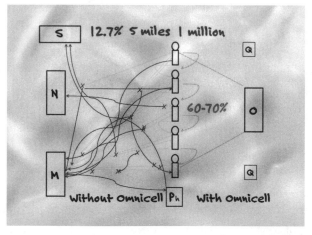

Courtesy of Omnicell.

And what impact would this have on patient satisfaction?

Imagine the right side of this diagram showing you how things would be different with Omnicell.

With Omnicell, your nurses can access the medication cabinet remotely, from any computer or workstation in the unit. [Draw dotted lines from patient bed to O rectangle.]

They won't have to go all the way to the cabinet to request or waste medications, which minimizes all the back-and-forth that makes them more vulnerable to interruptions and distractions, and can cause medication errors.

In a sense, what you're doing is giving them the ability to create their own personal "quiet zones" [draw Q boxes] where they'll be better able to think through issues in a clinical way, so that they're less frazzled, less likely to make medication errors, and more focused on the patients instead of on all the other problems that are demanding their attention. It also means that nurses can significantly shorten the time between assessment and medication delivery, so they'll be able to get the patients what they need faster, with less disruption.

What about all those endless loops around the hospital that hurt efficiency and increase the likelihood of interruptions?

When you install Omnicell's SinglePointe software solution, you'll be able to keep everything your nurses need for their patients in a single, secure location—right here in the cabinet. The system profiles virtually 100 percent of the medications that a patient might take and assigns them to secure drawers by individual patient. This way, you can effectively eliminate instances of nurses having to stop what they are doing and hunt for missing items. This keeps them focused and on their task and better able to concentrate on patient care.

Better yet, you can also implement our Mobile Medication System, so that your nurses can transport medications right to the bedside in a secure, locked-drawer cart. This not only speeds up medication delivery and reduces steps around the unit that increase the risk of interruption, but also gives the nurses one more opportunity to double-check the MAR to make sure that everything is in order. [Draw dotted lines from patient to patient.]

This goes a long way toward alleviating the stress and anxiety that cause depression and burnout in nurses—and they'll be more satisfied with their jobs because they're doing what they became nurses for: taking care of patients.

That's why hospitals and health-care facilities that have made patient satisfaction their top priority are coming to Omnicell. They know that if they can focus their nurses on patients, not problems, they'll enhance patient safety. They know that if they can give nurses back their time, they'll improve nursing efficiency. And they know that if they can just let their nurses be nurses, they'll increase nurse satisfaction.

What kind of effect could this have on patient satisfaction?

Well, a study by Kaiser Permanente shows that when nurses spend 60 to 70 percent of their time here, in direct patient care, safety and outcomes are dramatically improved. That's what hospitals come to Omnicell for. By simply letting their nurses be nurses, they can make significant improvements in patient satisfaction.

With this simple visual, Omnicell's salespeople can easily tell the story of how the company helps its customers provide better care to their patients.

Some Additional Tips for Creating Big Pictures

Don't tell yourself that you're not creative enough to come up with your own Big Pictures. You don't have to have the "creativity gene." Big Pictures are about problem solving. Anyone can create a Big Picture, but you'll never get there if you think you need some obscure type of talent to do it. We've seen people who are engineers, scientists, or accountants—i.e., people who don't normally think of themselves as being creative—come up with very effective Big Pictures.

Don't come up with something that requires you to be good at drawing. If your drawing requires you to be an artist, it will fail. When you're talking to a customer, you don't have time for art. Use simple shapes—stick figures, circles, arrows, pyramids, and so on—to create your Big Picture.

Think with your hands. Big Pictures can be challenging to come up with. They will almost never come to you if you just sit at your desk and think real hard. You need to put pen to paper. Just make some scribbles as you talk through your customer's challenges and how you can solve them. Your Big Picture will start to emerge after a couple of passes.

Work with a friend. This exercise benefits from an initial flow of ideas, regardless of whether they are good or bad. You need to just start the flow going. Partnering with someone helps a lot. And you can end up with something that you both can use.

You've learned how to use number plays and what-if-you questions to grab attention. You've seen how you can use customer stories with contrast and props to wake a slumbering brain. You've learned how to use Big Pictures to simplify the complex and make abstract ideas concrete.

But, if you were going to master only one technique, this next technique would be the one to pick. It will have the greatest impact on your personal income, the job opportunities you're offered, and your ability to influence people in your personal life.

CHAPTER 14

Personal Stories, Metaphors, and Analogies: The Key to Liking

A few years back, Erik was in Seoul airport waiting for a plane to take him to Kuala Lumpur, Malaysia, to deliver this work. As he waited, he noticed that a large number of people were wearing the type of mask you see doctors wearing during surgery.

It was the height of the SARS scare in Asia, and the fear was that SARS could spread easily from person to person. What's interesting about SARS, though, is that it wasn't originally spread by a "superspreader," i.e., someone like Typhoid Mary. Instead, when the first SARS victim was in a hospital, a doctor mistakenly hooked him up to an aspirating machine, which blew the victim's SARS-infected breath into the air.

Were it not for that mistake, SARS might never have passed from person to person and become an international issue. It's not that the virus wasn't powerful. It was. It was just that something else had to happen to make it easy to spread.

The same thing is true of your message—your story. If you want to make it easy to spread, you need to do whatever you can to make it spread easily. (But your message will be for the good of your customers, not like SARS.)

All the techniques in this book help with the core problem of making your message easy to spread. Yet, this next technique, when executed well, is probably the most powerful of all of them. It's called *personal stories*.

Personal stories are like an aspirating machine that takes your message and makes it transfer easily from person to person. Why are personal stories so powerful? In part, it's because you have positive associations with people who share stories with you.

How far back in your life can you remember someone sharing stories with you? If you're like most people, you can remember back to a time when you were a young child, and a parent, grandparent, or loved one read stories to you.

In fact, the only memory Erik has of his great-grandmother is sitting next to her on the couch, because she was too old and frail to let him sit on her lap. He remembers her hands, because they were so different from the hands of anyone else he knew at that time. They were very thin and bony, with raised-up veins. And he remembers her telling him the stories of Peter Rabbit and Benjamin Bunny.

He also remembers that she never once opened a book to tell those stories. She'd told them to so many generations of children that she could tell them from memory.

The point is that you have positive associations of people who share stories with you.

Share Stories, not Data

Another way to think about it is like this. When you get together with friends, do you share data?

No. You share stories. Stories are how you talk to people you like.

But what about when you're around people you don't like? Do you take the time to share stories with them?

No. If you don't like someone, you keep the conversation transactional. You finish up and go on to the next thing.

So, the question is, do you treat your customers as if they're people you like? Or do you treat them as if they're people you don't like?

When sales professionals prepare for conversations with prospects, they usually focus on getting all of the facts straight about their offerings. And certainly, you need to be accurate in what you say about your solution.

But you also need to connect with your customers. You need to treat them as if they're people you like. And the best way to do that is through stories. These aren't the customer stories with contrast that you read about earlier. These are personal stories that tie into your message.

Stories Create "Liking"

Robert Cialdini is considered the world's most famous researcher on human influence. His book *Influence: The Psychology of Persuasion* is required reading for marketing students in colleges and universities. He says that one of the most powerful ways to influence people is through a concept that he calls "liking."

You may think it's obvious that people buy from people they like, and you're right.

If that was everything Cialdini had to say on the subject, he wouldn't be famous today. What was surprising about Cialdini's theory of liking was not that people buy from people they like. It was that people buy from people that they think *like them*.

In his book, Cialdini tells the story of the most successful car salesman that ever lived. Joe Girard's performance was so remarkable that he won the title "Salesman of the Year" for GM for 12 years straight and was described by the *Guinness Book of World Records* as the "world's greatest car salesman."

Joe took extreme advantage of the liking principle. Every single month he sent each of his 13,000 customers a holiday card that had the name of the holiday, his name, and one message: "I like you." As Joe explained, "There's nothing else on the card. Nothin' but my name. I'm just telling 'em that I like 'em."

So, how can you communicate to your customers that you like them? You could do something as extreme as Joe, or you could take another approach that also tells your customers that you like them.

You could treat your customers the way you treat other people you like. You could treat your customers the way you treat your best friends. You can share stories with them.

As you read earlier, most sales professionals prepare for a sales meeting by getting all their facts in order—their *i*'s dotted and their *t*'s crossed. In the process, they forget to talk to customers in the most basic way that humans talk. They forget to tell stories.

Once you start sharing stories as part of the way you talk to customers, you'll see relationships change. Your customer relationships will be deeper and more rewarding. Your customers will also share stories with you.

How to Tell Stories in Selling

In the context of sales messaging, you want your stories to tie into the benefits that your product delivers. Your stories should have a purpose. (This isn't to say that you shouldn't share personal stories that just come naturally when you are talking to a customer. Those are great, too. The idea here, though, is to learn how to use personal stories to support your message.)

Part of the power of using personal stories in your messaging is that doing so naturally reduces the Old Brain's resistance. A good story captures the mind and takes you on a journey.

Here's an example of how one of our students used a personal story to break down his prospect's natural resistance to change.

Here was his scenario. Imagine that you're in his shoes.

You are selling a complex software solution that brings a lot of value to a company, but that also requires the company to change its existing processes.

You may find your customer asking you to change your system to work with her company's "old" processes.

However, doing that often causes the customer to lose key advantages of using your system.

How can you get your customer to see that, instead of making the system work with her old processes, she should instead take advantage of the power she will get from the new way your system will work in her business?

This was the challenge this salesperson was facing. Here's how he chose to break down his customer's resistance with a personal story.

Today, you are going to see a system that will help you reduce your costs, increase your revenues, and gain a competitive edge. But like most new systems, it will also require some changes in the way you do business. And sometimes people want to stick with their "old" processes because that is what they are used to. Whenever I think about this natural reaction, it reminds me of something that happened to me a while ago.

When I was going to Boston University, I drove a two-door Honda.

It was a great car, but since I was a poor college student, it didn't have power anything. So, if I wanted to roll down the window, for example, then I had to *roll* [does hand motion of rolling down the window] down the window. And if I wanted to roll up the window, then I had to *roll* up the window [does hand motion again].

Like I said, it was a great car, and that wasn't a problem. But at some point, the latch on the inside of the driver-side door broke. So now, if I wanted to get out of the car, what did I have to do? Well, I had to *roll* down the window and stick my arm out to open the door from the outside door handle.

It was a pain at first, but I quickly got good at it. In fact, if you've ever been to Boston, you know it rains a lot. Well, I got so good at this that I could roll down the window, stick my arm out, and open the door so fast that I wouldn't get much, if any, water on my sleeve [does arm motions].

And it snows a lot in Boston, too, and the snow heaps up on the sides of the car. But I got to where I could roll the window down, stick my arm out, arch it over the snow, and open the door without getting any snow on my sleeve [does arm motions again]. So, the car worked for me.

But then I got married. And then we had our son, and he turned four years old, and my wife said that this two-door Honda wasn't cutting it any more. So, we decided to get a minivan.

As we were driving to the dealership to look at minivans, I told my son that if he fell in love with one of the minivans, he shouldn't let the salesperson know it. I didn't want him to destroy daddy's negotiating power.

So, we get to the dealership, and my wife and son are inside a few of the vans, and my son comes out of one and whispers, "Dad, come here."

He's whispering because he doesn't want the salesperson to hear what he's saying.

My son whispers, "Dad, you've got to buy this minivan." I ask why.

And he whispers, "Dad, you've got to buy this minivan. This thing is awesome!" I ask why again. What's awesome about it?

He says, "Dad! You won't believe it! Inside there's this button. And when you push it, the window automatically goes down. *And then you can stick your arm out the window and open the door!* [If delivered well, this gets a big laugh.]

Now this is a fun story, but you need to tie it back into your message, so you might say something like:

You know, we can all be like my four-year-old son sometimes. We get used to seeing something done a certain way, and we think it is the best or the only way to do it. But sometimes technology comes along that makes things better, and we need to change the way we do things to get the most out of the new technology. That's what you are going to see today.

This is just one example of how a personal story can support your message and help you connect with your prospects and customers.

Metaphors and Analogies

Another unique thing about stories is that they have more flexibility and applications than any other messaging technique.

Erik considers himself to be a pretty good cook—not world-class by any means, but he has learned to cook a few things that he's proud of.

One evening, he was over at his friend John's house, and John served him some chili that he'd made that day. It was *really* good. (John later won a chili contest with the recipe, so it's fair to call it award-winning chili.) Erik tried to figure out what was in it that made it taste better than other chili that he'd made himself or eaten somewhere else. Finally giving up, he asked John, "What did you put in here that makes it taste so good?" And John said, "Chocolate."

Erik wasn't expecting that.

The interesting thing was that, even when you knew that there was chocolate in there, it was hard to detect. Yet it gave the chili a surprising depth of flavor that made the whole thing better. Leaving the chocolate out would have robbed the recipe of that little extra something.

Of course, chocolate by itself is pretty great, too. It can be a dessert on its own. It can be just a featured ingredient in a dessert or the literal icing on the cake.

Or it can be subtle, as it was in the chili, making a contribution, but not being obvious.

Stories can be used in sales messaging the same way. You can use a story as a Grabber. You can also use a specific type of story—a metaphor or an analogy—as a way to subtly improve and bring depth to another message object.

For example, the Hammock that you read about earlier in the book is a combination of a Big Picture and a metaphor.

First, we created the visual by graphing how much of a message is remembered. Then we stepped back and asked, "What does that graph look like? What would make it more memorable?" And then, someone came up with the idea of calling it "the Hammock" because it's shaped like a hammock, and this also ties in with the point of the Big Picture—that your presentation can put people to sleep.

The use of the Hammock metaphor takes an already effective Big Picture and makes it better, deeper, and more memorable. It's the chocolate in the chili for that Big Picture.

Words in Common

Another use of metaphors is to combine them in an unexpected way to create a new perception in your customer's mind. This technique is called *words in common*. (Consider it a bonus Grabber technique.)

Imagine that you sell software that affects many departments in a business. You need to present to a roomful of executives who are trying to decide which vendor they'll use for this solution. For this exercise, assume that your company name is ABC. You put up on a flip chart three words:

- Secretariat
- Lance Armstrong
- Companies that use ABC

Then you say,

Secretariat, Lance Armstrong, and companies that use ABC. What do they all have in common? [You'll hear people say things like, "They're all winners."]

That's true. But there is something else that they have in common. They all have an unfair competitive advantage that's invisible to the naked eye.

For those of you who are not familiar with Secretariat, he was perhaps the greatest racehorse in U.S. history. He won every race in the Triple Crown, the three big races that greatness is judged by. Not only did he win each race, but he won the last one by 31 lengths, destroying his competition.

When Secretariat passed away, an autopsy was done at the University of Kentucky. And what it found was that Secretariat's heart was almost two-and-a-half times the size of the average thoroughbred's heart. The average horse's heart weighs 8.5 pounds. Secretariat's heart weighed 22 pounds. He simply had a better, more efficient engine than his competition. He had an unfair competitive advantage that was invisible to the naked eye.

As an up-and-coming cyclist, Lance Armstrong was tested at a clinic in Texas to see how he compared to other athletes in his field. What the clinic found was that Armstrong's heart was about 30 percent bigger than the average man's heart and his lungs processed oxygen twice as efficiently as the average person's. He simply had a better, more efficient engine than his competition. He had an unfair competitive advantage that was invisible to the naked eye.

What does all of this have to do with companies that use ABC?

Well, a recent study done by [insert prominent third-party name here] showed that companies that use ABC have a 4 percent greater return on assets than companies that don't use ABC. They simply have an unfair competitive advantage that's invisible to the naked eye. And that's why companies are coming to us for these solutions.

Contrast this approach with simply putting up a bullet point on a slide that says that a particular study shows that our customers get a 4 percent greater return on assets. Which approach will be more memorable after you leave the room?

And look at the connections that this approach creates. You get to connect companies that use your solution with multiple winners. When used properly, words in common is a great way to take advantage of stories to make your message stick.

So, you can use personal stories to connect with your prospect. You can use metaphors and analogies to make your message more memorable and give it depth, often in a subtle and powerful way. You can also combine the two and use your personal stories as metaphors to make a point about your solution.

Here's how one student of this work did just that.

He was selling a solution that did "exception report-ing." It would look at data from a bunch of different places, and could create a report giving just the "exceptions"— the points where the data showed that something unusual might be happening. At the time, this feature was unique to his system. His competitors would just give you all the data, with no exception filter.

Here's how he decided to message this advantage with a story.

> When I was a teenager still living with my parents, we lived on the bank of a river where people were allowed to do "net fishing" at certain times of the year.
>
> What we would do is stretch a net from one bank to the other. Then, after we had waited some period of time, my dad and I would pull the far end of the net over to the bank we were on. The net would be too heavy to pull up onto the shore. Sometimes, it would have as much as 1,000 pounds of fish in it.
>
> So, somebody had to wade into the water, grab the fish by hand, and throw them up onto the riverbank. Not surpris-ingly, my dad felt that I was the best person for the job.
>
> So, I'd go wading into this water that was boiling with fish. And there'd be fish slapping at my legs [uses hands slap-ping on pants to simulate the fish]. But the reality is, that didn't bother me. They were just fish. They couldn't hurt me.
>
> But every once in a while, somewhere in the water inside the net, I'd see a head rise up out of the water, about the size of a fist [holds fist up to paint the picture]. And it was the head of a snapping turtle.
>
> And if I didn't see that snapping turtle, I might reach the wrong way and risk losing a finger or part of my hand.

So while I didn't care about where the fish were, I did care about where the snapping turtles were.

Now, why do I mention this? Because it's a lot like your business today.

You're surrounded by information that is coming at you from all sides. But most of the time, that information isn't telling you anything important. It's just telling you that everything is operating the way it should be. It's like the fish hitting my legs—not anything you need to worry about.

What you need is a report that shows you where the snapping turtles in your business are—those places where something's gone wrong, and you need to do something about it.

That's what our exception report provides you with. It gives you a way to see those snapping turtles, so that you don't get hurt.

You can bet that that salesperson's story and point were remembered.

As you build your overall solution story, look for opportunities to use these smaller personal stories to make your message come alive, help you connect with your customer, and talk to your prospects as if they're people you like. (Hopefully, you do like them.)

You'll learn still more techniques for creating and delivering a simple, differentiated, and memorable message. But before you do, it's time to learn *why* you need to do these things.

CHAPTER 15

Old Brain vs. New Brain: Messaging for a Decision

You are being asked to do a lot of things you may not have done before—find your Power Positions; use Grabbers; create Big Pictures; tell stories with contrast; use props; use personal stories. You might be wondering, is all this really necessary? This chapter is devoted to showing you why these techniques aren't just "nice to haves," they're "must haves" if you want to message for fast, easy decisions.

As you learned in Chapter 9, in a simplified view, the brain is divided into three primary areas:

The *neocortex* (the wrinkly part) is like the brain's computer; it loves to process data, and it will do so all day long and be happy doing it.

The *limbic system*, which sits underneath the neocortex, is where all emotions reside—love, hate, and all the other varying shades of human emotion.

The *brain stem* and other older brain structures, which Robert Ornstein describes as the *Old Brain*, are responsible for your survival.

Why should you care about the Old Brain when it comes to your sales messages? Because science shows that the Old Brain is the *filter* through which all decisions are approved.

The question then becomes, why should that be the case? The neocortex is more powerful than any computer ever made. Humans have the largest neocortex in the animal kingdom. It's one of the unique things that separate us from other animals. Why wouldn't the neocortex be in charge of decision making?

Think about it this way. Imagine that hundreds or thousands of years ago, some of your ancestors left their cave or mud hut or some other dwelling and headed down to the local watering hole.

Suddenly, on the path in front of them, there appeared a tiger.

Did your ancestors say to themselves, "Isn't that interesting? I wasn't expecting a tiger here today. You know, I've never been this close to a tiger before, so I never noticed that the orange stripes go all the way around, but the black stripes don't. And look at his ears. They're pointed right at me. And look at his eyes. They're looking right at me, too. Isn't that interesting . . ."

Obviously, your ancestors didn't react that way. Instead, their Old Brain took over, and they ran. And because they ran, they were able to pass their genes down from generation to generation. If they hadn't run, you wouldn't be reading this book right now, because you wouldn't be around. So, the Old Brain dominates decision making because survival is of the utmost importance.

If the Old Brain dominates decision making, what appeals to the Old Brain? There are seven key things that have been shown to impress the Old Brain. They are

- Emotion
- Firsts and lasts
- Contrast
- Visuals
- Simplicity
- Making it personal
- Concrete

You'll find that all the things you've been taught so far appeal to one or more of these areas.

Emotion

Getting some emotion into your message is the key to making your message memorable. In fact, your Old Brain uses emotion to mark things that are important enough to be remembered.

Jim McGaugh, a professor and fellow at the Center of Neurobiology of Learning and Memory at the University of California, Irvine, has spent years investigating what it takes to make a memory last. One of the ways in which he and his colleague, Larry Cahill, test this theory is by conducting studies in which people look at slides with varying emotional content—things like a picture of a snake or a decomposing dog.

Then, while the subjects are viewing the slides, the experimenters make each viewer stick one of his arms in a tub of ice water. The reason they do this is that ice water is known to trigger an emotional response in humans. When they test the subjects a week or two later, the experimenters find that the subjects can remember the more emotional slides better. That emotional response made the subjects' memories stronger while those memories were still forming in their brains.

So, what does this mean for you? Well, you could try bringing a bucket of ice water with you on your next sales call, but assuming that this isn't practical, then what it means is that you need to get some emotion into your message if you want your message to survive after you leave the room.

Right here and now, you can test this idea that emotion helps your message survive after you leave the room. Grab a piece of paper and something to write with.

No, seriously. It'll be worth it. We'll wait.

(We're waiting.)

Okay, now on that sheet of paper, put a series of steps—like this:

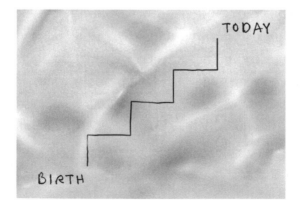

Now, take a moment, and on those steps write the things that happened between the time you were born and today that are most memorable to you. They could be things that happened to you personally. They could be things that happened to others. They could be world events. It doesn't matter. Just capture on those steps the three to five things between the time you were born and today that are most memorable to you.

(Don't jump ahead yet. Really try this. Then, read on.)

If you were to see this done by a roomful of people, no matter where you are in the world, you would see certain things come up consistently on this list. Things like

- Birth of children
- Wedding day
- Divorce
- Graduation
- First day of school
- 9/11
- Berlin Wall coming down
- Hitting first home run
- Death of a loved one
- Hometown team winning a championship
- Getting hurt somehow (car accident, falling off your bike, or something similar)
- Meeting your spouse or significant other for the first time

Do the things on your list match any of these?

What's interesting is that every time people put a list like this is together, there are a few things that the lists have in common. The first is that these events are highly emotional moments. Another thing that the events in these lists have in common is that often they're things that happened a long time ago, yet the person making the list can remember those moments very vividly.

However, if you were to be asked what you had for lunch a week or two weeks ago, you'd probably have to struggle to remember what you ate. (Unless it's a routine, such as you always have three martinis for lunch, or unless something significant happened.)

Yet you can remember the events you put on your list very vividly, and that's because they were emotional.

There is something else that you'll see consistently in these lists. Not necessarily every item on the list, but most of them, will be examples of firsts and lasts (beginnings and endings)—graduation, wedding day, birth of children, and similar events. You're going to look at that next.

Firsts and Lasts

Your Old Brain is also strongly influenced by firsts and lasts, beginnings and endings. A clear example of that is shown in the Hammock. That is why you want to start with a Grabber early in your message. It's also why you need to close *hot*.

Don't end with the typical phrase, "Any questions?" Instead, say, "You've seen how, only with us, you can do (Power Position 1) and (Power Position 2) and (Power Position 3). So, where do we go from here?" Be direct and make it pop.

You can see this vividly in the research concerning the Hammock, which you heard about earlier in the book. As your prospect's Old Brain is exposed to something new (like your message), it needs to make an assessment: "Will this information help me live longer, or might it kill me?"

So, what do you think the Old Brain decides pretty quickly when the lights go down and the PowerPoint goes up? "I've seen all this before. This isn't going to help me live longer, and it isn't going to kill me. I can safely go to sleep for a while." And then it stays asleep until it hears those magic words that come at the end of a meeting and spike the Old Brain back up out of the Hammock: "in conclusion," "in summary," or something similar.

Your Old Brain is constantly on the alert for the unexpected—things that break the pattern that it's used to. It doesn't pay much attention to things that happen the same way every time. That means that your first big opportunity in your messaging is to take advantage of the time when the Old Brain is naturally paying attention—the beginning of your message.

You can see the lesson of the Hammock played out in many areas besides sales messages. If you are as old as Tim and Erik, you might remember that once upon a time, Tuesday nights at 8 o'clock meant *Happy Days* and *Laverne and Shirley* were going to be on television. The first three or four minutes of those shows were the same every week. There was the same theme song, the same scenes playing in the background, and the same credits. Then there was a commercial break. After the commercial break, the show would start. At the end of the show, there were still more credits, and then nothing more until the next week. And it wasn't just those shows; every show started and ended with that same formula.

We used that time to get a snack, go to the bathroom, or finish a chore, knowing that we wouldn't miss anything good until the commercials were over.

That's not how it's done nowadays. Makers of TV shows have learned the lesson of the Hammock. Think of how your favorite TV shows start. They get right into the action. They don't make you sit through credits and then a commercial before the story starts. That's because they know that they need to get you engaged as quickly as possible, or you'll change the channel. And most shows don't just end with credits anymore. They often have a short scene after the end credits are done, or sometimes teaser scenes for the next week's show or the show that immediately follows. The point is that the producers of TV shows know how precious those beginnings and endings are, and they take full advantage of them.

Contrast

The Old Brain also loves contrast. And the closer together the things being contrasted in your messaging are, the more powerful the impact will be.

The power of contrast has been tested in many ways. One study had students at a college campus rate the attractiveness of "normal" people in pictures on a scale of 1 to 10. A second group of students rated those same people, but there was one difference in their test: before rating the "normal" people, the second group of participants was shown pictures of a bunch of supermodels. Can you imagine what happened to the attractiveness ratings that this group then gave the "normal" people?

The ratings given the "normal" people by the second group went down dramatically. However, a third group of participants was also tested. This group was shown the supermodel pictures a full hour before they saw the pictures of the "normal" people. The impact of that hourlong gap was that the participants rated the attractiveness of the "normal" people the same as they would have rated them if they had never been shown the supermodel pictures at all. The point is that contrast is important, but you need to show the contrast close together for it to have impact.

In your messaging, the contrast that you want to create is to show your prospects that staying where they are today is an "unsafe" decision and moving to your solution is the "safest" decision. That's how you get the decision maker, the Old Brain, to choose your solution. Your challenge is that your prospects often feel safer doing nothing than doing something.

Your prospects are like the frog that is placed in a pot of water at room temperature. If the temperature of that water is raised slowly enough, the frog will sit there until it boils to death, even though it could easily jump out. However, if you took that same frog and threw him into a pot of already boiling water, he'd jump out immediately. What causes the difference between those two scenarios? Contrast.

(Before we explain more, please don't test this theory on frogs. It's just an analogy, people.)

When the frog is in the pot of water that starts at room temperature and slowly gets warmer, moment to moment he feels safe. He might notice that it's getting a little warmer, but it doesn't seem like that big a change.

The frog that is tossed into the pot of already boiling water experiences a huge contrast between the air temperature and the water, and its Old Brain says, "Get me out of here! Now!"

Your prospects can be just like that frog. They've been living in their environment—the status quo—for a while, maybe years. Yeah, it's been getting a little worse over time, but they're used to it. And as long as they feel comfortable with their present situation, you've got no chance to sell them anything. The trick is to show them that where they are isn't safe. You need to show them that they're sitting in a pot of boiling water.

Another important thing to understand about people is what motivates them. If you ask people which is more motivating for the average person, to move away from a bad thing or to move toward a good thing, you'll hear different guesses. Happily, you don't have to guess because there's good scientific evidence around this question.

What the science shows is that people are about twice as motivated to move away from a bad thing as they are to move toward a good thing. This is based on something called *prospect theory.*

Daniel Kahneman and Amos Tversky are giants in the field of decision-making research. They developed prospect theory as a way to show how people evaluate choices when they're making a decision.

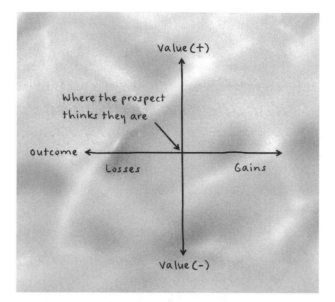

Assume that the center of the graph, where all the lines intersect, is where your prospect sees his situation before you meet with him. If you talk to him about how you can help him go to a better place—in other words, move him along the S-curve up and to the right—he will see value in that.

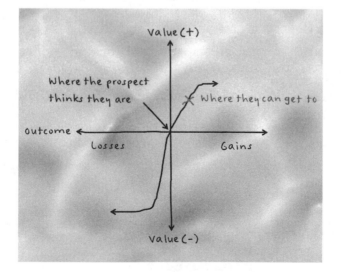

But notice the angles of the S-curve. It moves more steeply downward when going to the left than it moves upward when going to the right. In other words, if you can show your prospect that his starting point is not the comfortable intersection of the lines, but instead he is farther behind than he realized, it provides far more motivation to change than simply showing him how much he can improve things.

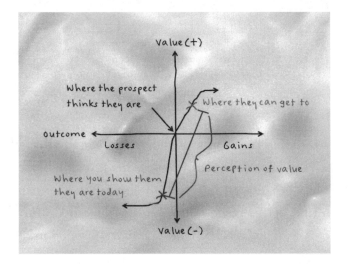

And when you can do both—show the prospect that where he is is not a great place and then show him that where he can get to is a much better place—you dramatically increase the amount of value the prospect will see in your solution.

That's why, when you're using the customer story with contrast technique, you're told to do the customer "before" story and then immediately do the customer "after" story. You do this for the same reason that you need your Big Picture to show the prospect's world without your solution and then immediately follow it up with your prospect's world with your solution. It's because of the way the Old Brain works and the way the Old Brain perceives value.

Visuals

Of your five senses, the Old Brain responds most strongly to the *visual* sense. In fact, processing things that you see takes up about half of the resources of your brain, with the other half being devoted to everything else. You learned some of the science behind this in the earlier chapter on Big Pictures and the pictorial superiority effect.

Why would this be the case? Think of it in terms of survival. Imagine this scenario:

Congratulations! Your friends have had a vote and decided that you are the best person to go hunt down a man-eating tiger in India. You're a lucky person to have won such respect from your friends.

There is only one catch: you get to take only one of your five senses with you.

Are you going to take your sense of taste? Probably not, because if you can taste the tiger, the tiger can taste you.

What about your sense of touch? Same problem. Smell? That's not going to work.

What about your sense of hearing? Tigers are pretty quiet.

Obviously, you would take your sense of sight. For hundreds and thousands of years, vision gave your ancestors enough warning time to allow them to escape danger before they became lunch. That's why it dominates for the Old Brain.

So, which techniques can help you reach your prospect visually? Obviously, Big Pictures and props. They take your solutions and make them something that your prospect can see. That's what makes them powerful.

Again, you're being told to use these techniques, not to make you work harder, but because this is the way the decision maker, the Old Brain, works.

Simplicity

Robert Ornstein, father of the Old Brain concept, did a study in which people were intentionally overloaded with too much information. What he found was that if you overload people with too much information, there are four specific behavior changes that you can expect to happen in the people who are overloaded.

1. *Can't respond.* One thing that happens is that people get to the point where they can't respond anymore. It's almost as if you see doors closing behind their eyes. (Sometimes you can even see their eyes close as they fight off going to sleep.)
2. *Irritated or bored.* Also, people who are overloaded with too much information go into one of two emotional states: either they get irritated or they get bored. Can you imagine two worse emotional states to put your prospect in? You know you need to engage your prospect at the emotional level, but those aren't the emotions you're going after.

3. *So what?* Another thing that happens to people when you give them too much information is that they start to develop a "so what" attitude: "So what?!? Why are you telling me all this?"

4. *No decisive action.* But the worst thing that happens when you overload someone with too much information is that he can no longer make decisions. And that's a killer when you're trying to sell something.

Have you ever been working through a sales cycle in which everything seemed to be moving along just fine, but then your prospect went silent for a while? Maybe he stopped returning your calls and e-mails? And then sometime later, when you finally do hear back from the prospect, it turns out that, while you haven't lost the deal to the competition, the prospect has decided to put off the decision for a few months, or maybe until next year.

You didn't lose that deal to your competition. You lost that deal to no decision. So, what happened?

The Old Brain is a relatively simple mechanism. It can be easily overwhelmed. When it gets overwhelmed, it can no longer see clearly that it will get X results if it does what you are recommending.

And when it no longer can picture exactly what results it's going to get from moving forward with your solution, what becomes the safest thing for the Old Brain to do? Nothing. Its safest move is to just keep doing what it's been doing all along.

Yet, how do most salespeople respond to a confused buyer? They give the buyer more and more information . . . and that doesn't help.

Just as Babe Ruth's initial instincts (Chapter 1) were that he'd get better results from swinging the heaviest bat he could, a salesperson's instincts often tell her to give a prospect as much information as possible. After all, if the prospect knew as much as you do about your solution, wouldn't he have to buy it? Unfortunately, it doesn't work that way.

Your Old Brain craves simplicity.

A year after the Flip Video camcorders hit the market, they had a 13-percent market share in the camcorder market. They made that huge leap without much in the way of advertising. Their growth came mainly from word of mouth. They also got that market share with a product that did almost nothing compared to its competition.

It had only a 2X zoom. It had only three buttons—one to record and stop recording, one to play a video, and one to trash a video. It wasn't HD. You couldn't take pictures with it. You could go on and on with the list of features that it *didn't* have, compared to its competition. So, what made it so successful?

According to David Pogue, tech writer for the *New York Times*, who was comparing the Flip to other simple electronics products that took the market by storm, the Flip was *so simple, your mastery is immediate, and so is your sense of pride and happiness.*

You can think of other products on the market that are simple and a joy to use compared to others in their space. That doesn't mean that the underlying technology is simple or that the underlying business model is simple. It just means that the experience for the customer is simple. And people (and the Old Brain) love simple. Simple feels safe.

So, how do you simplify your message? You don't have to tell your prospect about everything your solution can do. You can just focus on those things that are different about your solution compared to the solutions that your competition offers. You focus your message on your Power Positions. You can make your message simple by using Big Pictures that make it easy for your prospect to see how your solution affects his world. You can also make things simple for your customers by using metaphors and analogies, because they allow the Old Brain to move easily from something that it understands to something new.

Again, you're being told to do these things to make it easy for your prospect to buy from you. A confused buyer cannot buy. Make it easy for your prospects by doing the work ahead of time to simplify your message.

Making It Personal

Earlier you read about the importance of you phrasing, but most salespeople have been taught to use we phrasing. They do this because they want to communicate to the customer the idea that the relationship will be a partnership. It won't be the rep versus the customer. It'll be more like a marriage—walking arm in arm down the aisle together. The problem with this is that it doesn't work for the Old Brain.

Your Old Brain cares about survival, but whose survival does it care about? Its own. It's not worried about anybody else's survival.

Your Old Brain lives by the adage that if you and a friend are walking through the jungle and you see a tiger, you don't have to be faster than the tiger. You just have to be faster than your friend.

The problem with we phrasing is that it's ambiguous. Who do you mean when you say "we," anyway? Do you have a mouse in your pocket? Do you mean yourself and the people back at your corporate headquarters? Do you mean yourself and anyone from your company you brought with you to the meeting? Do you mean yourself and the prospect?

And because it's ambiguous, we phrasing doesn't work for the Old Brain.

In fact, once you start paying attention to it, you'll notice that we phrasing just sounds strange. It's not the way you talk to people that you like.

Another subtle and powerful thing about you phrasing is the way it forces you into your customer's world. It's impossible to use you phrasing if you don't really understand your prospect's business objectives and pains. And when you show that you understand the prospect's world, it changes the way he views you.

One of the simple ways in which the Old Brain views you is as either "part of my tribe" or "part of other." If you are seen as "other," you're going to have a tough time persuading your prospect. Think of your prospect's Old Brain as constantly asking the question, "Is this person going to bring food into my cave or take food out?" How do you think most salespeople are viewed?

Use you phrasing to keep things personal for your customer and to show that you're part of his tribe. His Old Brain will love it.

Concrete

You learned earlier that your prospect is more motivated by concrete things than by abstract ideas. One of the tools that can help you make your message concrete is Big Pictures. Props also help by taking something intangible and making it tangible.

Here, however, you'll see a special focus on numbers.

Salespeople love numbers—the bigger, the better. There are some challenges with numbers, though, particularly related to the Old Brain.

A few years back, we did a survey of some of our top clients to see what type of return on investment (ROI) they were getting from working with us. The news was exciting. The ROI was 5,000 percent. That's not a typo.

One of our sales reps decided to use this in a number play. He gathered up numbers showing the different ROIs you would have received if you had put your money in different investments during the previous year. It looked something like this:

2 percent	Savings account
4 percent	Money market fund
12 percent	Stock index fund
323 percent	Hottest stock of the last 12 months
5,000 percent	Investing in Power Messaging training for your staff

He asked for advice before using this message with clients. The advice he heard was this—don't use percents.

It's not that percents are always bad. They are not. You've seen us use percents in various spots in this book.

It's that people just can't wrap their minds around 5,000 percent. What does that really mean? First, it just sounds unbelievable. The Old Brain can't grasp it or accept it. Also, a lot of people can't do the math needed to translate that into real numbers. They just get confused.

So, the coaching he got was to do the number play, but to present the numbers this way.

How much would $1 be worth now if you'd invested it one year ago in a few different investment categories?

$1.02   Savings account
$1.04   Money market fund
$1.12   Stock index fund
$3.23   Hottest stock of the last 12 months
$50.00 Investing in Power Messaging training for
        your staff

It's much easier for your Old Brain to grasp that if you invest $1, you can get a return of $50 than it is for your Old Brain to understand that 5,000 percent ROI means the exact same thing. In both cases, it also helps the Old Brain to see the numbers contrasted with those for other investment options.

Another thing that can either help or hurt the concreteness of your message is your choice of words. The Old Brain likes simple words that have clear meanings. Don't use jargon or words that could mean many things, if you can avoid it. Keep your language simple, and the Old Brain will like it.

Seven Things That Impress the Old Brain

Back to the original point of this chapter, you're hearing from us that you need to use Power Messaging techniques to create a message that works for the decision maker, the Old Brain. Every technique you've learned here applies to at least one of the seven things that have been proven to impress the Old Brain.

- Emotion
- Firsts and lasts
- Contrast
- Visuals
- Simplicity
- Making it Personal
- Concrete

You've learned how to find your story (Power Positions), make it come alive (Grabbers), and show how you'll get the results you promise (Big Pictures). Next, you need to look at how you're going to prove your claims.

CHAPTER 16

Proof: It's Not Just Numbers

What's truer than the truth? The story.

—OLD JEWISH SAYING

You've learned how to find your story. You've learned techniques for getting your prospect's attention and creating a Bed of Nails to avoid the Hammock, so that his Old Brain won't fall asleep. You've got the prospect leaning into your message. You've learned the science behind why this is necessary. The next thing you need to learn is how to prove your claims in the most powerful way.

This is another area where a salesperson's intentions are often great, but his instincts lead him in the wrong direction.

Many salespeople believe that if they can just show the numbers—the return on investment (ROI) that a prospect can expect from their solution—those numbers will be so compelling that the customer will have to buy. They believe that everybody is motivated to do whatever she can to maximize the dollar return on investment. It's a curiously common belief, given all of the evidence to the contrary.

Do you have a 401(k) plan at work? Are you enrolled in it? The answer to that last question is dramatically affected by the way your company handles enrollment. If your company makes you fill out paperwork to get enrolled, then only about 20 percent of your fellow employees will be in the 401(k) plan. If, instead, your company makes you fill out paperwork only if you *don't* want to be in the 401(k), then 90 percent of your peers will be enrolled in the plan.

So, 90 percent versus 20 percent—that's a huge difference in participation in something that makes a life-changing difference in your financial future. Taking 15 minutes of your time to fill out the paperwork can give you a return of hundreds of thousands of dollars when you retire. It's a no-brainer. If money drove decision making to anywhere near the extent that most sales professionals believe, there's no way that this statistic would be true.

A big part of the reason that salespeople believe that ROI is what ultimately causes someone to buy is because that's what their prospects tell them, right?

Prospects don't say, "Get me caught up in a story that helps me feel pain if I stay where I am and feel gain if I move to your solution, and I'll buy anything from you." Instead, customers say, "Any decision to buy will be based on the numbers. We need hard facts and data to prove that your solution works."

In actuality, it doesn't quite work that way.

We were running a messaging workshop recently, and the attendees were talking about how to get a customer to make a buying decision in your favor. A CFO raised his hand and said, "It all comes down to money. You just need to show your customer how you will help his bottom line."

Many of the folks in the room nodded their heads at this comment. So we asked, "Have you ever had a situation in which your client agrees that he should move forward with your solution? That it makes financial sense? But he keeps putting things off month after month after month?"

Now even more heads were nodding. "Why does your client do that if he knows that each month he puts off the decision, he is losing money that he can't get back?" Now people looked unsure. They'd all experienced it, but they weren't sure why it happened.

The reason that happens, we told them, is that the customer feels more emotion around the money, time, and resources that he'd have to invest to move to your solution than he feels around the financial gains that he would eventually get from your solution.

The CFO fell into the trap that too many salespeople fall into. He believed that people use logic and self-interest as the primary way they make decisions. He believed that if a decision could be reduced to money, then it would be made logically. He fell into the same sales trap that kills many sales cycles.

Even When It's All about Money, It's Not All about Money

Most people believe that everyone is motivated by money. Salespeople, in particular, often feel strongly about this. After all, their entire incentive structure is built around pay for performance. If you were given free money, with no strings attached, you'd take it, right? Anybody would, wouldn't they? It's the rational thing to do.

Scientists tested this assumption using something called the "Ultimatum Game." In the Ultimatum Game, there are two people who play. Player A is given $100. Player B has none. Player A has to offer some of her $100 to Player B.

Player B can either accept Player A's offer or reject it. If Player B accepts the offer, then both Player A and Player B get to keep their respective money. If Player B rejects the offer, neither gets any of the money.

Player A gets to make just one offer. There is no negotiating between the two.

Logic says that even if Player A offers Player B only $1 and Player A gets to keep $99, Player B should accept the offer, because even $1 is better than nothing. However, that's not what happens.

This game has been played around the globe, and what is striking is that Player B usually rejects Player A's offer if the offer is less than 30 percent of the overall amount of money (in this case, $30)

Amazingly, this is true even if the amount of money offered was worth two weeks' salary to Player B. The 30-percent threshold stuck.

Now, think back to the CFO's comment. You can see that this doesn't fit his model of how people make decisions. He would expect Player B to accept Player A's offer every time, no matter how much or how little it was. But that's not what people do. People do not rely purely on logic for any decisions, even ones that seem as logical and obvious as "taking free money."

So, why is it that the CFO and so many salespeople get this wrong? Everyone makes decisions every day. Certainly, you know from your own experience how you make decisions, right?

Feel vs. Real Syndrome: Don't Fool Yourself

There's something that golf instructors refer to as "feel vs. real." One of our consultants, Mike Miller, went to a golf instructor a number of years ago. Mike had been playing for a while, but he wanted some additional help. After watching him swing a few times, Mike's instructor said, "My goodness, you must be some kind of great athlete."

Mike was surprised at the comment. "Why do you say that?" he asked. The instructor said, "Because your backswing and your downswing are so out of line, it's amazing that you can hit the ball at all!"

Mike laughs today as he retells the story, "I thought I was swinging the club like Tiger Woods, but then the instructor videotaped me, and I saw I wasn't even close."

In golfing, the concept of "feel vs. real" means that you might feel as if you've got the perfect golf swing, but reality is often very different. When you are swinging a golf club, you are staring at the ball. You don't see your backswing or your downswing. You have to try to feel them. But you don't have any reason to be good at feeling your golf swing. It's not something that your survival depends on, and if your survival doesn't depend on it, evolution doesn't give you that ability.

This is why even Tiger Woods, perhaps the greatest golfer in the world, has a swing coach. He's no more immune to the pitfalls of feel vs. real than you are. In the same way, feel vs. real explains why people have trouble believing that emotion plays an important role in all decision making, including decisions about business solutions.

Timothy Wilson, professor of psychology at the University of Virginia and author of the book *Strangers to Ourselves: Discovering the Adaptive Unconscious,* says that scientists used to believe that the unconscious mind is like an iceberg and the conscious mind is like the tip of the iceberg above the water. He says that many of today's scientists now believe that the scale of that image is off. If you imagine the unconscious mind as an iceberg, the more appropriate scale would be to imagine your consciousness as only a snowball on top of that iceberg.

The conscious mind is tiny compared to the vast amount of functioning that is carried out by the unconscious mind. In addition, Wilson says that the functions of the unconscious mind aren't accessible by the conscious mind. It's as if the unconscious mind operates behind a closed door that the conscious mind can't open. As a result, you don't have good access to information on why you make decisions.

You might be able to come up with a story to justify a decision, but there's a lot of influence coming from parts of your brain that you just can't access. All of this means that when your prospect says that she's going to make her buying decision based on hard facts, she is not deliberately lying to you. In fact, she thinks that she's telling the truth. But you need to know that it's going to take more than just facts for you to win.

No Emotion, No Decision-Making

Antonio Damasio has led research in the field of the impact of emotion on decision making. His work was influential in helping us to see that emotion is a part of all decision making. Part of his inspiration for studying the connection between the two was the remarkable story of Phineas Gage.

In 1848, Phineas Gage was in charge of a railroad-building crew that was laying down track in Vermont. One part of his job was to blast away rock that was in the path where the crew wanted to lay track. He did this by drilling a hole into the rock and filling the hole about halfway with an explosive powder. Then he put a long fuse in the hole and poured sand into it until the hole was filled almost to the top.

The sand needed to be compacted, or "tamped," to create enough pressure so that when the lit fuse reached the powder, the explosion would go into the rock, as opposed to just blowing out the top of the hole. The tool he used to tamp the sand was a metal rod, slightly bigger around than a broom handle. It weighed more than 13 pounds and was more than three feet long.

On this sunny day, Phineas was doing just that. He drilled the hole, poured in the powder, and placed the wick in the hole; then, before his partner poured in the sand, Phineas was distracted for a moment.

After the distraction passed, he grabbed the iron rod and drove it into the hole to tamp the sand. However, his partner hadn't put the sand in yet. The rod struck rock, creating a spark and causing an explosion.

The rod exited from the hole and caught Phineas just under his left cheekbone. It proceeded through the top of his head and landed more than 80 feet away, covered in blood and brains.

His shocked coworkers ran to him. They found him lying on his back looking up at the sky. He was still alive and still conscious.

He recovered from the accident and lived another 13 years. He was 25 when the incident happened.

One of the challenges for scientists who study the brain is that often the only way to find out how the brain works is to study someone with a damaged brain. The Phineas Gage case has been studied by many scientists for more than 100 years. It was Damasio who made the connection between Gage's accident and the impact of emotion on decision making.

The remarkable thing about Phineas was that in many ways he was the same person after the accident as he had been before the accident. His memory was intact. His ability to speak wasn't affected by the accident. He could still do most of the things he'd always done at the same level as before the accident—reading, writing, math, and the like.

Yet, he was different. This once very capable man, a man who was respected by his peers as a person with good judgment, started to show very poor judgment. He seemed to have no sense of how his actions or words at a given moment might affect his life later. He said whatever came to his mind, somewhat like a person who's had far too much to drink and starts saying things that he would normally keep to himself.

When Damasio studied the case, he began to wonder whether Gage's behavior changed because the "high" regions of the brain, where complex decision making took place, were now separated from the "low" regions of the brain. Damasio's theory was that Gage's Old Brain was separated from the more advanced portion of his brain. This meant that emotion and feeling, which occur in the Old Brain, were no longer connected to the part of his brain that assessed how different scenarios might play out in the future.

In other words, rather than hearing a warning that if you say this or that to your boss's wife, you might not be employed anymore, he didn't have any emotion around the potential future consequences of his actions. As a result, he behaved as if there were no consequences beyond whatever he wanted in the present.

The implication of Damasio's theory was that if you separate emotion from decision making, then decision making breaks down.

Rather than separating emotion from decision making being a good thing, you actually need emotion to guide you in making good decisions. Further, the impact of emotion on decision making often happens at an unconscious level, but it's always there. The idea that you can simply remove emotion from decision making and make a rational or logical decision is false. The only way you could do that in real life is if you had damage to your brain.

When Damasio tested his theory with people who had damage between the emotional parts of their brain and the long-term planning parts of their brain, what he found validated his theory. The people with that specific type of brain damage could no longer make decisions regarding the future. If you asked them what they would do tomorrow, they couldn't answer. They didn't know how to decide.

When emotion was separated from the future planning part of the brain, all possibilities looked the same. No possibility felt more right or more wrong than another.

The Impact of Proof Points

You've been told that people buy on emotions and then justify their purchase with facts. We all do this. You couldn't buy purely on logic if you wanted to. Our brains just don't work that way, regardless of the stories we tell ourselves.

So, what does this have to do with proving your claims when messaging?

One of the most common mistakes sales professionals make when selling is that they lead too early with proof. They believe that all they need to do is use the brute force of facts and logic in their pitch, and the prospect will buy from them. What you need to understand is that proof has its place. But it should come only after you've created the emotional momentum in your prospect that makes him want to move from where he is to where your solution can take him.

Use Grabbers and Big Pictures to create that emotional momentum to change. Then, use proof to help his Old Brain feel safe moving forward with you.

What can you use for proof? Let's look at the most obvious type of proof first.

Third-Party Statistics

Third-party statistics can be very effective. However, they need to be fairly recent if they are to have impact. They also need to be from a credible source. They are most powerful if they are about your company's solution and the pain you solve, as opposed to being just general industry statistics, at least when it comes to proving your claims. General industry statistics often don't point prospects to your solution above all others. When you're at the proof stage, though, you want the proof to be about your solution, not a generic statistic about the problem that you solve.

You are probably already comfortable using third-party statistics. If you're like most sales professionals, you just wish you had more. So, where can you find them?

Our experience is that there is usually someone in your organization who is responsible for staying on top of what analysts are saying about the industry and about your company. Ask this person what she has that you can use in your sales efforts. If there isn't someone in your company who is assigned to tracking analysts' comments, the next best bet is to check with high-level management. They're often on top of analysts' comments, because these comments can drive Wall Street's perception of the business. It's amazing how many times we've found good statistical proof just by asking the right people.

Once you have those third-party statistics, you should pair them up with a story about one of your customers who got the results the third party refers to. You want to show that those results are ones that you can produce. A customer story (discussed later in this chapter) is the best way to do that.

Return on Investment Calculators

These are often mistaken by sales professionals as proof sources for your claims. They're not. If a prospect still needs convincing about the impact of your solution, a return on investment (ROI) calculator won't get them there. ROI calculators make a lot of assumptions out of necessity. If a prospect isn't already convinced that she needs what you're selling, she's going to challenge all the assumptions in your model. For an ROI calculator to work as a proof source, it needs to be paired with the next type of proof source.

Customer Stories

Unlike when you are using customer stories as Grabbers, customer stories used as Proof points don't need quite as much storytelling. When you are using a customer story as a Proof point, you can get away with just using the customer's name and going through the results they got from your solution.

Contrasting before and after results is still important here, but you can make these stories a little shorter. In fact, listing the names of two or three customers and the results they produced using your solution can be enough to convince a prospect that you can do what you claim.

When you pair two or three customer stories with an ROI calculator, the calculator tool instantly becomes more believable. You'll get less resistance concerning the assumptions in your model.

Demos

A demo can be a powerful way to prove your claims. Seeing a piece of hardware or software do what you claim it does can be an effective Proof point. However, you do need to keep in mind that prospects are often skeptical that the ease with which your solution works in a demo will prove to be the same when they need to use it in "real life."

That's why you should treat demos in much the same way as you use ROI calculators. Always pair demos with two or three customer stories that support the claims that you are trying to prove with the demo.

One thing you will have noticed by now is that the best proof is often a customer story. This chapter starts with an old Jewish saying: "What's truer than the truth? The story."

This saying refers to the idea that just telling someone a set of facts doesn't always feel convincing to that person in the same way that a story does. Don't push too hard on facts at the expense of customer stories. Customer stories are the most convincing Proof points you have.

What about Technical Demos?

Having said that, when you are selling technical products, it's almost impossible to avoid doing a technical demo at some point in the sales cycle. If you never need to do a demo to sell your solution, you can skip to the next chapter. If you do need to do demos, this section is for you.

One of the first challenges with technical demos is that the people delivering them treat the actual product demonstration as the "body" of a presentation. They start by pitching at the beginning of the message, followed by giving a technical demo that then lasts anywhere from 30 minutes to 3 days (we're not joking about 3 days; we've coached organizations that do demos that are as long as 10 days), and then wrap up by trying to close the business at the end. That's a poor model for messaging.

When a demo goes on that long, it can quickly move from a sales message to a training session on how to use the product, even though the prospect hasn't yet decided that he wants to buy. Your demos should never feel like training. They should be Proof points that support your Power Positions.

Another challenge with demos is the inherent risks. You know about the technical risks of having the product fail during the demo, but that's not what we mean here. You need to be just as worried about the risk to the prospect's vision of how the solution will work.

Your prospect has an image in his head of how the solution will look and feel. That vision will be just a bit off in some form or another. The prospect hasn't seen your product yet, so his image is his fantasy of how your product will look, how the tasks will flow, and how it will affect his day. Every screen you click to, every feature you show, will be at least slightly off from his fantasy. The more you show, the worse it gets. Every click is a risk to your closing the deal.

Introducing the Cooking Demo

This is why, when you have to do a demo, you should do a *Cooking Demo.*

A Cooking Demo borrows from the demo model you see on televised cooking shows. Think about the way they work. When the cook shows up in the kitchen, the ingredients are already sitting there, chopped, measured, and sitting in little glass bowls all around the stove. Then, the cook takes all the ingredients and puts them in a pan. Then, he takes the pan and puts it in the already preheated oven. And what's the very next thing he does?

He takes an already cooked version out of the oven. He doesn't make you sit there and wait the 30 minutes to 2 hours that it might take the casserole to cook. That's the idea behind a Cooking Demo. Don't make the prospect sit through every little step before showing her the magic report or piece of information that she'll be able to get out of the system. Get her to that end point as quickly as possible.

Another thing to keep in mind is that just because you are doing a technical demo doesn't give you permission to bury your customer in the Hammock. The person doing a technical demo is often someone other than the sales rep for a given opportunity. Technical demos should be integrated into your message, not treated separately. Grabbers and Big Pictures should be used to set up the different areas of the demo that you will use to prove your claims. You need to do everything you can to create spikes before, during, and after the demo. And make sure you remember to use you phrasing throughout.

Add a Mini-Drama

Lastly, the best demos aren't just a series of facts. The best demos create an experience. One of the most effective ways to do that is with a technique called *Mini-Drama*. A Mini-Drama is done by showing a day in the life of your customer without your solution, and then contrasting that with a day in the life with your solution.

There are many ways to do a Mini-Drama. Here's one example: Imagine that you're selling a system that helps salespeople keep track of where orders are in process and also lets them know if there's enough stock of an item to meet a customer's request.

The prospect you're working with doesn't have a system like that. He keeps track of everything through paper. You might do something like this:

This is a day in the life of Joe down in sales. It's Friday at 4:30, and this call comes in.

[Grab your cell phone and act as if you're taking a call.]

This is Joe. Oh, hi, Mr. Smith. [Get out of role for a minute and tell your prospect, "He's my largest customer. If it wasn't for him last year, I wouldn't have made quota."] What can I do for you today? Oh, three days ago you ordered 5,000 widgets. Okay, umm, I should have a printout of that. Umm. Okay. Oh, you need them switched. Okay. Let me get a pencil. Umm. What do you need done? Okay. You need 2,500 of 'em shipped to Texas. Okay. And 2,500 to Oakland. Okay. Umm. I'm not sure that they're still here. Umm. Let me put you on hold for just a . . . time is money, yep yep, no no, that's not a problem. I'm going to call down to Tony on the dock. One minute. You got it.

[Puts customer on hold. Dials warehouse.]

Tony, please be there, please, please, please. Tony? Voice mail. Yeah, you have a nice day, too, pal. Hey, Tony, yeah, this is Ted. I'm up here on extension 224; I got Mr. Smith on the phone. I need to find out if the 5,000 widgets left for Texas because if they haven't, you need to call me back. I need to redirect them, so please call me. All right.

[Hits button on phone to get back to Mr. Smith.]

Mr. Smith, yes, I've got Tony down in the docks researching this right now. Uh-huh. Oh. You need 2,500 of those that are going to Oakland to be Widget B not Widget A, like you typically order. Okay. Let me see, I've got my manufacturing report. Umm. Here it is. Oh, wait, that's last week's date. Umm. Let me put you on hold. . . . No. No. Yes, sir. Fast. But it's not a problem. Just one more hold. Okay.

[Tell your prospect to imagine it's 10 painful minutes later. Then proceed with the Mini-Drama.]

But I've got some more . . . But they'll be . . . But you . . . No. All right.

Well, just call me back if you change your mind. Thanks.

[*Note:* This was the "before" part of the Mini-Drama. Now, you make the transition to the "after" part.]

That's the life of your salespeople today using your current solution. Here's how it would be different using our solution.

It's the same scene, Friday at 4:30, and you get the same phone call. The only difference is, now you have the right tools.

This is Ted. Oh, hi, Mr. Smith, how are you? Oh, you're calling to check on an order. [Starts doing a Cooking Demo as he pretends to handle the call.] Okay. Last four digits of your full number are 8400, if I remember; is that correct? Yep. Great. Yes, I see that you ordered them three days ago. They're on the docks ready to go. Oh, you want to make a

221

change. What do you need done? Okay, so instead of 5,000, you need 2,500 to Oakland. I understand. Do you want those to the Brisbane address or the Sacramento address? You got it. Not a problem. And what else can I do for you today? Oh, 2,500 of those that are going there need to be Widget Bs. All right, let me find out what we have in inventory. Okay. You need 2,500. . . . I have 300, but the good news is that I've got a whole bunch coming in next week. Will the 300 hold you over? Great. I'll go ahead and add those to your order. Super; now I did notice here that you haven't ordered any of your Widget Ds in almost nine weeks. How are you doing on those? Oh, Okay, you'd like to get those. Great. I'll go ahead and put those into the same container as the 300. . . . We'll eat some shipping. Oh, by the way, the price has come down; it looks like about 7 percent. Yeah, that's a nice little savings.

Oh, this weekend? No, we're going skiing. Oh, are you, too? Oh, excellent, we should get together for a drink. Love to.

Hey, thanks a lot for the order. I'll see you soon.

Thanks.

Your Mini-Drama then concludes:

Now, that's a much nicer world, isn't it?

Well, let's be clear on a couple of things. It's not the people; you have the talent and the ability.

It's not the effort; everybody works hard.

But it's the tools that enable you to do what you need to get done every day.

That's the power of ABC software.

What you've just done is create a story that your prospect can live in. She can see how her world will be affected by moving to your solution. It's a powerful way to use a demo to convey your message.

One last point on Mini-Dramas: Whom do you think a Mini-Drama reaches best? The user? A mid-level manager? A senior-level manager?

Most people guess that they work best for the user, but what we've seen teaching these techniques for over 20 years is that the person they reach best is the highest-level manager in the room. Why? When you do this well, at the end of the Mini-Drama, the most senior person in the room will turn to everyone else and say, "Is it really like that today?" And if you did it well, people will say, "Sometimes it's even worse."

Now, thanks to the Mini-Drama, the senior manager, who is normally shielded from the day-to-day hassles of the operation, feels the pain of this problem much more than she ever did before.

CHAPTER 17

Words, Voice, and Body: Message Delivery Matters

One of us, we won't say which one, watches the reality TV show *American Idol*. A few seasons ago, Katherine McPhee was one of the final three contestants on the show. She did a poor job during one of her songs, and now it was time to hear from the judges. Randy Jackson and Paula Abdul told her that she'd done a bad job, and now it was Simon Cowell's turn to give feedback.

Simon made a similar negative comment in his own acerbic way, and then he wrapped up by saying, "If I'm being honest, I think that was your best performance of the year." Now, he hadn't meant to say *best*. He'd liked her much better in previous performances. He'd simply misspoken.

Now Katherine was supposed to do her short interview with host Ryan Seacrest. As Ryan was asking her what she thought of her performance and the judges' feedback, Simon kept trying to interrupt them. Finally, in frustration, Ryan asked what Simon wanted to say. And Simon said, "Somebody just told me that I'd said that this was

Katherine's best performance of the year. But that's not what I meant to say. I meant to say that it was her worst."

Ryan and Katherine looked puzzled and then said, "You did say it was her worst performance." But he hadn't. He'd said, "Best." But because of his voice and body language, they'd heard what he meant to say. They didn't hear his actual words.

There is a lot of good research concerning voice tone and body language, and it confirms things that most people intuitively believe about how communication works. And it gets to one of the central ironies of delivering a message. When preparing a message, most people spend all of their time focused on the words they'll use and spend no time thinking about their body language and voice tone.

Unfortunately, these findings have often been used to prescribe presentation solutions that don't quite work. Many presentation skills courses take this information and emphasize the importance of getting your body language right and eliminating nervousness in your voice. They focus on nonverbal aspects of messaging without giving much attention to the words you say.

What you'll hear from us is that both what you say (verbal) and how you say it (body language and voice tone) are important. Focusing too much on nonverbal aspects can create just as many problems as focusing too much on the verbal part of your message.

So far in this book, you've spent a lot of time on how to get your message right, figuring out your Power Positions, and how to make sure the story you tell is one in which your customer is the hero.

You've learned how to use Grabbers and Big Pictures to present your Power Positions in a way that is compelling and memorable.

However, we'd be remiss if we didn't include a chapter on some of the more traditional nonverbal messaging skills, specifically voice tone and body language—but, like everything else in the book, with an updated and integrated point of view.

You Need to Make Sure That You Connect

Take a look at these numbers. What do you think they mean when it comes to delivering your message and connecting with your audience?

78 percent
89 percent
56 percent

78 percent is the frequency with which a communicator believes he is clearly communicating his message when using e-mail.

89 percent is the frequency with which the receiver believes he is interpreting the message correctly when reading e-mail.

56 percent is the frequency with which the receiver interprets e-mail correctly.

These numbers show that when you take away voice tone and body language, you end up with a poorly received message. The absence of voice and body language in written communication is what makes things like writing an e-mail so difficult. It's why people use emoticons in e-mail and text messaging. (*Emoticons* are the clever use of punctuation that shows your emotion.) It's also why sometimes people will write "sarcasm off," meaning that the previous sentence or paragraph was meant to be read in a sarcastic tone, but now you're going to be serious.

Body language and voice tone add depth to your communication. But not only that, when your words are out of sync with your voice tone and body language, the listener puts much more weight on your tonality and nonverbal behavior.

It's the 7 percent–38 percent–55 percent rule.

This research was done by Albert Mehrabian, professor emeritus of psychology at UCLA. What he found was that when people are talking about their feelings or attitudes, the receiver of the message will trust what she thinks the communicator's tone and body language are saying more than she will trust the words the communicator is saying.

In fact, the receiver will get 55 *percent* of the message from body language, 38 *percent* from voice tone, and only 7 *percent* from the actual words the person used.

It might not seem obvious at first, but when you think about it, you see why nonverbal elements would dominate when you are talking about feelings or attitudes. Imagine that a friend of yours was walking across the room toward you. His head is down. His shoulders are slumped. He's moving very slowly and shuffling his feet. When he finally gets to where you're standing, you ask, "How are you doing today?" And he says, "Great."

Do you believe that he is doing great? Obviously not. Everything about this person's body language told you that he was having a lousy day. And you're going to believe that body language over his words every time.

Imagine another scenario. You're talking to a friend on the phone. This friend usually has an upbeat, chipper tone to her voice. But during this conversation, she's got an Eeyore-like, woe-is-me tone to her voice. Again, you ask, "How are you doing today?" Again, she answers slowly with a deep sigh, "Great." Which are you going to trust more, her words or the tone of her voice? Obviously, her tone will be dominant for you.

Presentation Skills Training Misses the Point

There are presentation skills courses out there that will teach you what to do with your hands, how to make eye contact, how to stand next to the projection screen (making sure that you turn three-quarters toward the audience and point at the screen, but don't touch it, because that will cause it to ripple and create a distraction . . .).

These presentation training classes also will drill you until not only don't you say *umm* and *ahh* anymore, but you almost can't. They believe that if these presentation mistakes in your voice and body can only be fixed, you will be able to deliver the perfect presentation.

Here's the problem. When you focus on how you say every word and how you deliver every gesture, you can give a polished presentation. But you'll often fail to do the thing you should be focusing on most of all. You'll fail to connect with the people you're conveying your message to. You've completely eliminated any authenticity.

As an example, for most people, it takes a lot of concentration to focus on removing *umms* and *ahhs* from their speech. When they are successful at it, the problem is that they no longer talk naturally. They start to sound like robots. They've polished off the edges so much that they seem just a little less human. And that doesn't help you connect to your prospect.

At the same time, if you don't believe the words that are coming out of your mouth, if you don't believe your message, you are still going to reveal that lack of conviction through your body language, no matter how much you practice your delivery.

The reason this happens is that there are aspects of your body language and voice tone that are simply beyond your ability to control for any meaningful length of time. These are what Alex (Sandy) Pentland calls *honest signals*.

Honest Signals

Professor Pentland is the director of Living Labs at MIT. He has spent years and conducted thousands of hours of studies examining how people communicate with one another. He talks about what he's learned in an excellent book called *Honest Signals*.

It's the broadest, deepest research on nonverbal communication available. One area of his research focuses on the impact of nonverbal signals versus words. What he has learned is that there is an *unconscious* communication channel between people, one that reveals itself through nonverbal signals.

Because these honest signals happen mostly at the unconscious level, they are very hard to fake. They are tied to your biology and are very difficult to suppress. Honest signals are things like the speed and consistency with which you speak. If you are wrestling with conflicting ideas in your head, it's very hard to maintain consistency of emphasis and pacing when you speak, and that's what makes it an honest signal.

When your level of interest in something increases, your body naturally gets more active. You want to move, if only by bouncing your leg up and down or fidgeting with your hands. You may be able to stop yourself from doing it, but it takes a lot of concentration. The fact that you are concentrating on suppressing that honest signal will make all of your behavior less natural. This will, again, send an honest signal that you are trying to mask something. The receiver's unconscious will pick this up, and that disconnect will color everything he hears from you.

The opposite of an honest signal might be a smile or a firm handshake. Those are easy to fake, and as a result, at the unconscious level, the receiver doesn't really trust them. While you aren't always consciously aware of the impact that someone else's honest signals have on you, if you think about it the right way, you can recall times when honest signals from someone else have affected you.

Have you ever met someone and felt that something wasn't quite right about your interaction with him? You may not have been able to put your finger on it or articulate it, but you felt that something was just off? That's the impact of your unconscious finding the other person's honest signals to be inconsistent with his words. The effect can sometimes be subtle and other times more obvious, but honest signals have an impact on every human interaction.

By monitoring honest signals, Professor Pentland can accurately predict certain behavior. As an example, just by listening to the consistency of emphasis in a decision maker's speech and monitoring his body language, he can predict with near-perfect accuracy whether the receiver will buy what the person delivering the pitch is selling.

He can do that without knowing the actual content—the words—of the sales message.

Consider this experiment, which was conducted as part of the honest signals research.

Forty-two MBA students, split about evenly between men and women, at MIT's Sloan School of Management were given an opportunity to pitch their business plans to one another in preparation for a business plan contest. It was a great opportunity. All of the students had previous business experience, and the best plans were going to receive seed funding from venture capitalists.

As the pitches were delivered, the MBA students were asked to evaluate the others' presentations objectively. They were supposed to listen for things like: Was this business plan a good idea? Was it likely to be successful? Should it be funded? Did the market assumptions hold up to scrutiny?

At the end of each pitch, the students rated each presenter in three areas: persuasion, content, and style.

The first interesting result was the strong connection among the three. Even though the students were asked to evaluate persuasiveness, content, and style separately, in most cases, if a student rated a pitch high in one category, he rated the pitch high in the other categories, as well.

Pentland concluded that this shows that even people with a strong business background, as these students had, still can't separate style from content. The way you *deliver* your message appears to have a direct impact on the perceived *content* of the message.

Next, the same business plans that the students delivered to one another were given to venture capitalists to determine which plans would actually be funded. There were no presentations. The venture capitalists had only the benefit of reading the proposals. Interestingly, the venture capitalists chose a very different group of plans to fund from what the students chose.

What was the likely explanation for such different results? The students got more than just the written plans. They were also able to see the honest signals indicating how much each speaker believed in the plan. The venture capitalists didn't have that advantage. They had only the content, and that led them to very different choices.

This shows the power of your honest signals to influence the success of your pitch much more than the force of just an intellectual argument. (By the way, the venture capitalists were the ones who suffered as a result of not getting to see the pitches delivered. The data show that venture capitalists do a much better job of evaluating the potential success of a business plan if they can meet the people in person. That's why they almost always insist on it. They need to see the honest signals.)

The most surprising result of the entire experiment was the fact that Pentland was able to use equipment to predict with almost perfect accuracy which plans the students would vote to fund. The equipment based the decision only on monitoring the voice pacing, tone, and emphasis, along with the body language of the person doing the pitch. Again, he did it all without hearing or recording any of the actual words of the pitch.

Based only on the delivery style, his predictions of which plans would be chosen were almost 100 percent accurate. Why? Because he was monitoring the presenters' honest signals. And those honest signals have a powerful impact on the receiver of a message.

It turns out that the most successful "pitchers" talked at faster than a "normal" rate, and their emphasis was also consistent throughout their delivery. These are honest signals of enthusiasm for their ideas and confidence that their plan will work. This is only one example. Pentland's research is based on numerous studies that have led him to these conclusions.

You Can't Fake Confidence

Are you hearing us say that you should fake your confidence, so that people will buy from you? No.

What you need to do is become confident with your message first, and then it will come through naturally. It will keep your honest signals, well, honest.

How do you do that? This takes you back to the beginning of this book.

One of the reasons you need to do the work to find your Power Positions is to give you confidence in your own message. When you know what's different about your solution, and you know how to communicate that difference, your confidence naturally increases. And that starts to affect the honest signals that you give off. It's not about faking confidence. It's about giving yourself a basis for real confidence.

The next thing you need to do is put a little less burden on yourself. Don't give yourself an overly complex, abstract message to remember.

One of the things that make it hard for people to give off a sense of confidence is the burden that they put on themselves to try to "sound smart." They load their pitches with all kinds of complex, abstract language. They believe that using this kind of language will make their prospects believe that they are smart.

Does this actually work? We can confidently tell you that, no, it doesn't. (Erik wanted us to share one of his favorite *Dilbert* cartoons to drive this point home.)

Reprinted with permission from United Media.

This idea that "jargon is bad" was tested in a clever experiment, later published in *Applied Cognitive Psychology* magazine. Daniel Oppenheimer knew that undergraduate students often used complex words when writing papers in the hopes that they would impress their professors with how smart they are. So, he decided to test the impact of the use of complex words on the *reader* of the paper.

He used papers written in multiple versions, ranging from versions written with very complex words to versions written using very simple words. Then he had people evaluate how smart they thought the authors of the papers were.

The results were consistent across several runs of the study. The readers judged the authors of the papers written in simple language to be smarter than the authors of the papers written using complex words. The undergraduates' assumption that using complex words would make people perceive them as more intelligent was wrong. It's the ability to use simple language to communicate a complex idea that makes people think you're smart.

This ties back to our discussion on the Old Brain. The Old Brain craves simplicity. The Old Brain isn't going to buy your solution if it doesn't "get it."

Make it easy for your prospect, and make it easy for yourself. Use the plainest language possible when you talk about your solution.

Give Them Something Unexpected

Another thing to consider in your delivery of your message is how the choices you make affect the Hammock.

In many business-to-business selling situations, your prospect is expecting that you will, at some point, power up your computer and walk her through a PowerPoint deck. It's not that she's looking forward to it, but she does expect it.

And the lesson of the Hammock is that if you give your prospect's Old Brain what it expects, your prospect will stop paying attention. She may fake her interest, but her Old Brain will be focused on other things. You need to think about how you can break the pattern of what prospects expect.

One of the ways you might do that is by either not using PowerPoint at all or using very few slides when delivering your message. What if, instead of leaning so hard on PowerPoint, you used a flip chart or a whiteboard, or even a simple sheet of notebook paper to deliver your message?

At a minimum, you'd be breaking the pattern of what people expect, and that will help you keep the attention of the real decision maker, the Old Brain.

Another challenge with leaning too hard on PowerPoint is that people sometimes fall into a false persona when they start up a PowerPoint deck. They become "Presentation Man" or "Presentation Woman." And, subtly, everything about them changes—their tone of voice, their body language, and the words they use. They fail to connect. Their honest signals become less sincere.

A third challenge with using PowerPoint is this: Does your prospect know that you created your own PowerPoint slides? Not necessarily. Who might she think created those slides? Most people would say marketing. And they'd be right a lot of the time.

However, when you can deliver your message using a whiteboard or flip chart, or simply by turning a piece of paper toward your prospect and jotting down a few numbers or drawing a Big Picture, who gets credit for authorship then? You do.

And that automatically elevates you in the eyes of your prospect. You become more than a slide jockey. You get viewed as someone who can bring more of a consultative approach to their problems.

Don't Shy from the Jump

Here's one last consideration and piece of advice concerning this topic of delivery and words, voice, and body.

What's the modern Olympic event that's caused the most deaths and serious injuries? It's the events that pair a human and a horse—the equestrian events.

What happens is that a horse will be heading toward a jump, and at the last minute, it will either stop hard just short of the jump, throwing the rider over its head, or it will jump only hard enough to get partway over the jump, sometimes causing the horse to fall in a way that can break its leg or lead it to land on top of the rider.

What's strange about this is that the horse and the rider had already made lots of jumps of a similar size in practice, but for some reason, when the competition starts, the horse shies from the jump, and that's when things get dangerous. It's the failure to commit at that crucial moment that causes disaster for horse and rider. What does that have to do with messaging?

You've learned a new approach to messaging over the course of this book. You've learned how to find your story through your Power Positions. You've learned how to make the story be about your prospect through you phrasing and the hero model of storytelling. You've learned how to use Grabbers and Big Pictures to make your story memorable. You've learned the most powerful way to prove your claims.

Now it's time to deliver, and you've learned how your voice and body language affect the way your message is received. The only thing that will stop you from successful execution is failing to commit to the techniques.

If you go into your next meeting thinking, "Maybe I'll try this stuff, but first I'm going to feel out the situation," you won't be successful with your message. Your lack of confidence will come through in your honest signals. Your Old Brain will tell you to play it safe—don't try anything new.

And what will happen is that you'll shy at the jump. That's when messaging goes bad. That's when salespeople get hurt. That's when your opportunity dies.

There's a famous commercial with Michael Jordan, while he was still playing basketball, in which he says, "I've missed more than 9,000 shots in my career. I've lost over 300 games. Twenty-six times I've been trusted to take the game-winning shot . . . and missed. I've failed over and over and over again in my life. And that is why . . . I succeed."

In most cultures, it's a commonly held belief that people who are great at the things they do were born great at them. But every time you dig deeper, what you find is not that they were born great, but instead, that they decided that they were going to be great, and that they weren't going to let the first time they stumbled or tripped stop them from doing what they knew they needed to do.

You have just read several thousand words about the world's most powerful sales messaging techniques, and it would be a tragedy if you allowed that effort to go to waste out of fear that you might make a mistake the first time you tried these techniques. Don't allow fear to stop you from doing what you know you need to do. Don't allow fear to stop you from being great at delivering your message.

INDEX

ABOUT THE AUTHORS

Erik Peterson

Vice President
Strategic Consulting
Corporate Visions

Erik spends his time helping companies and salespeople around the world win at the three-foot level, when they're sitting across the table from their most important customers and prospects. Companies like GE, Amerisource Bergen, and Oracle have sought Erik's help in creating a simple, differentiated, and memorable story. He has delivered messaging skills workshops to more than 10,000 salespeople in 13 countries, and he leads a team that has delivered this work in 56 countries around the world. He has applied these concepts in selling situations as complex as selling multimillion-dollar, multiyear implementation solutions and in situations as straightforward as selling residential plumbing products in Germany. His clients describe the in-room experience with Erik, whether through consulting or skills training or keynotes, as the greatest learning event they've had in their careers.

Tim Riesterer

Chief Marketing Officer and Senior Vice President
Products and Consulting
Corporate Visions

Tim is a recognized thought leader and practitioner in the area of marketing and sales messaging. His first book, *Customer Message Management,* focused on increasing your marketing department's impact on selling by providing customer-relevant, sales-ready messages and tools that salespeople will actually use. Now, he's turned his attention to salespeople themselves and what actually happens when they are in front of the customer with their lips moving. Tim leads a team that provides consulting and training programs to align marketing and sales to create and deliver differentiated customer conversations. He's also a sought-after speaker and trainer on the topic, delivering keynote presentations for association conferences, analyst roundtables, executive forums, and corporate events.

ABOUT CORPORATE VISIONS, INC.

Corporate Visions, Inc., aligns marketing and sales organizations toward a common purpose—the differentiated, customer-focused conversation.

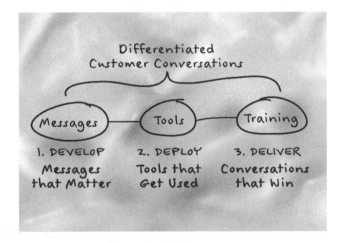

There are three keys to creating and delivering winning customer conversations. Marketing, Sales, and Training must work together to:

1. Develop messages that matter to your customers.
2 Deploy those messages in tools that get used by the field.
3. Train salespeople how to deliver the messages in an engaging and memorable way.

This unique methodology has been proven to work at companies such as ADP, CA, Dell, GE, Oracle, Xerox, and many others.

To see examples, get tips on messaging, and experience how customer-focused conversations can work for you, visit www.conversationsthatwin.com